Barnes & Noble Critical Studies

General Editor: Anne Smith

The Art of Malcolm Lowry

THE ART OF
MALCOLM LOWRY

edited by
Anne Smith

BARNES & NOBLE
BOOKS
10 East 53d St., New York 10022
(a division of Harper & Row Publishers, Inc.)

Barnes & Noble Books
Harper & Row, Publishers, Inc
10 East 53rd Street
New York

ISBN 0–06–496378–0

First published in the U.S.A. 1978
© 1978 Vision Press, London

Printed and bound in Great Britain
MCMLXXVIII

Contents

Introduction by *Anne Smith*   7

Preface: Malcolm—A Closer Look by *Russell Lowry*   9

1   *Under the Volcano*—The Way it Was: A Thirty-Year Perspective by *Richard Hauer Costa*   29

2   Tragedy as a Meditation on Itself: Reflexiveness in *Under the Volcano* by *Stephen Tifft*   46

3   Aspects of Language in *Under the Volcano* by *Brian O'Kill*   72

4   Malcolm Lowry and the Expressionist Vision by *Sherrill E. Grace*   93

5   The Own Place of the Mind: An Essay in Lowrian Topography by *George Woodcock*   112

6   "The Forest Path to the Spring": An Exercise in Contemplation by *Perle Epstein*   130

7   Intention and Design in "October Ferry to Gabriola" by *M. C. Bradbrook*   144

8   Strange Poems of God's Mercy: The Lowry Short Stories by *T. E. Bareham*   156

Notes on Contributors   169

Index   171

Introduction

Lowry is yet to become a respectably "established" novelist: critics still lament that Joyce had no successor in English fiction, and either pretend that the work of Lowry, who has a real claim to that title, exists somewhere on the freakish fringe, or dismiss it as merely the rambling "diaries of a dipsomaniac". But interest in his work is steadily growing, and with it, recognition of his tragic relevance to our own disjointed times. The contributors to this book seek to explore rather than to define that relevance, and to come, perhaps, a litttle nearer to the full appreciation of the genius they recognise in his work.

Edinburgh, 1978   A.S.

Preface:
Malcolm—A Closer Look

by RUSSELL LOWRY

When accepting the invitation to write an opener for this book I declined the accompanying opportunity to read some, or any, of the other contributions. This may seem to have been unwise—even impolite!—though I hope not, for my motive was simply to avoid the risk of muddying issues when the real objective was to clarify them. My role is basically practical and factual with here and there maybe a touch of plausible speculation. That of the learned essayists who have made the body of the work is critical, analytical, educational. I happen to know more than anybody about certain aspects of my young brother's life—but claim no place whatever in the world of scholarship. They, on the other hand, be they never so steeped in literary wisdom, can have known him only briefly, if at all, and have had to base many theories, deductions and conclusions upon supposedly autobiographical parts of his writings or, more dangerous still, upon second or third hand versions of equally dubious material.

No man is a hero to his valet—or as Plutarch (was it?) might have added—to his elder brother. So Malcolm is no hero to me, never was, never could be. But he has become a hero, or at least an object of much admiration and deep study, to thousands of people in many countries. Any who read this introduction may be assured that I have no intention at all of trying to "debunk" my own brother. Such an idea would be stupid, since he is an established figure who has already stood the passage of time and emerged with, apparently, a steadily growing reputation.

It must have been some sort of a presentiment that made me put on record fifteen years ago—in 1963 to be precise—in the hands of Liverpool's distinguished City Librarian, Dr. Chandler, a statement from which the following extracts are made. I still wouldn't change a word, so prospects of durability for the present extension seem reasonably good.

. . . I had little contact with (Malcolm) after the early 1930s by which time our ways of life, already divergent, finally separated.

Prior to that however we were extremely close friends as well as brothers. I was rather less than 4 years his senior, our other brothers being in turn 5 & 10 years older than me . . . but Malcolm and I as the juniors grew up in constant companionship particularly during the middle years of, say, 1915–25. It is of this period that certain aspects might well be clarified before too many false images are built up—images . . . not indeed without foundation but which give a very false impression of (his) basic character and background.

His work is now being taken as autobiographical. This is only fractionally true and the further back, the less. Some of the fragments and letters now being scraped together show this clearly (which) should be kept in mind when assessing material that may emerge in the future. . . .

Let me (deal with a few autobiographical incidents already published). . . . He describes various illnesses, accidents and experiences in childhood including eye-trouble—painful, disfiguring and involving long hospital treatment to avoid blindness, through parental neglect—a damaged knee, also neglected with crippling effect—and his "crucifixion" at eleven years of age as a Wolf Cub, at School.

True indeed, he suffered from ulceration of the cornea, at about 10, but was cured completely by a Harley St. specialist (name Hudson) to whom father took him when local treatments and doctors failed. Neglect? And he never entered or needed to enter any hospital during these years.

True indeed, he fell off his bicycle, with spectacular damage to one knee—but he was in the hands of an eminent local surgeon (name Paul) within an hour of the accident. Recovery was complete and left no physical handicap whatever. Malcolm was a pretty fair athlete in his own right. I know these things. I was there.

True indeed, he didn't like the Wolf Cubs—in fact he didn't like school. Period. But the symbolic crucifixion story is simply—symbolic. It simply doesn't add up. My brother Wilfrid and I were both at the same prep. school, quite a small one. My own closing terms there as one of the top kids covered Malcolm's first few terms. He certainly didn't get crucified then and by the time he was eleven (i.e. after two years)—if he was still a Wolf

Cub he'd be a pretty senior one—and well able to look after himself.

A much later incident . . . concerns the original appearance of *Under the Volcano* and his bitterness over lack of favourable family reaction. . . . This disregards the fact that being published in America, in days of dollar stringency the book was not available in this country . . . it also overlooks the difficulty of just what one says to a younger brother to congratulate him on progress towards drinking himself to death. Even in the sacred cause of Art!

These are examples of artistic licence, and I fear of alcoholic fancy built in after years around merely incidental grains of fact. But when the whole is taken as factual, gross distortion results not only of Malcolm's mental physical and artistic development —the latter now receiving so much attention—but also of the family background and atmosphere. In particular distortion of a father who though perhaps unimaginative and Victorian in his relationship with us all was certainly not neglectful. . . . Any notion of Malcolm as a tortured, neglected downtrodden genius during these years, is sheer nonsense.

Furthermore, it was thanks (if that is the appropriate word) to father's assistance that Malcolm was able to knock around the world as he did, picking up sensations, ideas, experiences and atmospheres—but also . . . sliding further and further into the volcano of his own creation. . . .

I have no desire whatever to take part in public comment— much less controversy, about Malcolm and having known and loved him well . . . as a live brother, I find no need to admire him as a dead giant. . . .

This document of which I have quoted one half or thereabouts was to be made available only to serious students. Maybe I buttoned it up too tight in my desire to avoid fatuous headlines in the local press. I needn't have bothered. Actually during the following dozen years only two "serious students"—how presumptuous can I get?—they were both Professors!—sought out this file, located only a couple of miles from The Birthplace, while the heavy brigade were combing the countryside for attributable clues.

The melancholy story of blindness and crippledom is quoted in the Bradbrook *Malcolm Lowry* and I vouch for the accuracy of that account. Now what on earth would make a man, on his own twenty-first birthday, in his own family circle, when asked for his earliest childhood memory, so strenuously avoid the obvious

—innocuous "Sunlight Soap", or "Castor Oil", or even "Your Big Blue Eyes Mama!"—and fire a salvo of grapeshot about his childhood having been one of perpetual gloom during which he was always blind, constipated, or a cripple? (Surely he just threw in the constipation to make the thing scan nicely, although a vague memory does linger of infant suppositories in a bathroom cupboard.) But what would, could, make him do it? I remember being pinned down by this question during an unscripted, unrehearsed film interview, and being unable to find a serious answer. On reflection since that baffling moment I have come to the conclusion that the only possible trigger-mechanism for an action so boorish and so uncalled for, was just sheer bloody-mindedness. And Malcolm found that it worked, from his point of view. It stopped the show (such as it was) and left him in the middle of the stage. Evidently he relished the impact produced by his statement, remembered it, and in years to come embroidered, extended and improved it. The image of the crucified genius was on its way. Had it occurred to him I don't doubt that his knee would have bled (accompanied perhaps by winkings of a blind eye) every 28 July, his birthday—or maybe on the anniversary of the phantom gunfight in Singapore!

Of his youthful sufferings Malcolm seems to have "used" only those with dramatic potential. Whether this process was studied or natural I do not know but, for instance, he says nothing about his longest-lasting and certainly not least distressing affliction— chilblains (very prevalent and apparently incurable in those days). He had about the worst I ever saw. In winter his hands looked like bunches of burst sausages. Almost unbearably painful—and itchy—at times, but lacking in dramatic appeal, although he cannot possibly have forgotten them. These chilblains quite certainly contributed to his awkwardness and so to his problems in other fields.

This drama/suffering ratio applies to the case of his celebrated "Autopsy", among others. He was "flayed at seven, crucified at eleven", with blindness and jeering thrown in for good measure! Well, he did indeed get an excessive whacking from one very temporary nanny when aged around three plus. At boarding school, nine plus, he probably had his leg pulled, as did everyone else. With me it was "gig lamps" for the hated spectacles. In his case it was probably his clumsiness, or more likely his bad temper, so easily baited. But who cares, and what is the difference twenty years later? One thing is sure, he was neither flayed nor crucified, figuratively or otherwise. So the trouble with the autopsy is that there's neither rhyme nor drama in it until you convert three and nine into seven and eleven, the only two numbers that will "go". From there on it's all downhill and the more picturesque the pain, the more brutal the torture, the better. This may be, and I hope it is, brilliant artistic creation and improvisation from very slight material. A rebellious child gets a whacking. A still rebellious, or bad-tempered, schoolboy gets his nose tweaked—or whatever. It has happened to millions. But there is only one Malcolm Lowry. If his writings are works of genius let them be recognized and admired as such, for what they are, rather than for what they are not. And the autobiography of my young brother is one thing they very definitely are not.

A long, and still steadily growing, string of legends is waiting to be demythologized, traced back and pinned into its proper place. Not, goodness knows, to discredit the man himself. He did his best in that direction and failed. What we want is a better idea of what made him tick, and why. During the years since that practically off-the-cuff document of 1963 I have spent many a winter evening chewing over these mysteries, turning up old photographs, papers, bits, bobs, and pieces. The problem at the moment is not how many to use, but how few can be made to serve the purpose.

Because it is harmless, illustrative, and to my knowledge has not been dealt with before, I pick on the Legend of the Schoolboy Golf Champion. Malcolm was a good boy golfer (I separate the words carefully)—he had a nice natural swing, which was strange because he was not a graceful mover, but there was nothing really exceptional about his game. I speak as one who played hundreds of rounds with him. In 1923 we both took part in an informal competition for sons and brothers, maybe friends too, of Royal Liverpool Golf Club members. I tore up my card, but Malcolm was round in 95 which won the under-fifteen age group. In 1925 he "shot" 88 and won the medal for boys between fifteen and eighteen. We were all delighted. But (and I have this in writing from the RLGC) this was no record, lower scores having been made in earlier years, and the event was in no sense a Championship. Arising out of this success brother Wilfrid, who was very much

13

our benevolent Mr. Fixit with Father, arranged for Malcolm to join a small local group on a trip to London for the real Schoolboy Championship. Off he went, to return sadly crestfallen, having "eaten something" and not been well enough to play. It all seemed slightly odd, but nothing more was said, the topic dropped out of sight and my impression is that he never played golf again. The whole episode would have been forgotten had he not revived it years later, with himself as the record-breaking Schoolboy Champ. I can only suppose that he was putting a patch over an irritating puncture in his self-esteem.

Years later still, talking to a notable Hoylake golfer and companion of many a youthful game I asked if he remembered what had happened to Malcolm on that trip. He did. Malcolm got so drunk overnight he couldn't he conveyed to the first tee, so, in effect, they propped him up in a corner until it was all over. The actual year of this happening is a trifle vague. It cannot have been the biographer's 1924, because the trigger event at Hoylake was definitely not until 1925. No matter, except perhaps as a pinpoint on early drinking.

That is enough for the present by way of demolishing purely "autobiographical" legends, though we shall probably find ourselves back on the theme. Malcolm himself was chief architect, of that there is no doubt. But he operated on a small scale, for his own amusement, or self satisfaction, or justification, call it what you will, and at the time he cannot conceivably have had any idea of the importance which would eventually come to roost on his slightest utterance—he was, oftener than not, covering his tracks, in the manner of shy people . . . and drunks. Certainly not laying a trail! And once the bloodhounds were after him, those who, as I said earlier, knew him not at all, or only briefly, found themselves on so many false scents that they, or most of them, simply ran round in circles. There is one deeply researched, documented, bibliographed and acknowledgment-spattered biography which contains at least ten crass mis-statements in the first three pages! In this atmosphere effects are attributed to non-existent causes, deductions are made from contrived evidence and still further conclusions are then based in a self-energizing spiral, on the original nonsense. The language moves further into the jargon so piercingly described by Dame Rebecca West as "academic pidgin English", and the reader is left stumbling about in a fog of abstract nouns. Malcolm himself undoubtedly started this process, but the commentators, the critics and the camp-followers have long since outdistanced their quarry. Malcolm must be laughing his head off.

Having got that off my chest it is time to deal with the lad himself, rather than his nightmare-image-in-a-broken-mirror. What was he like? As a child of, say, six (making me ten) he was chubby, blue-eyed, pink-faced, rather mousy-haired, a bit buck-toothed. He was a cheery soul, when not in a rage, and cheery again immediately afterwards. He wasn't very good at amusing himself and tended to lose and break things. Very generally speaking he remained like this for the next ten years, allowing of course that we both developed interests of our own, as well as those we had in common such as golf and collecting stamps. With the departure of the Nanny—the succession of cruel ones is fiction—he attended a local day-school and didn't like it, but after all one wasn't meant to *enjoy* school. Extraordinary idea! Then he came on to Caldicott—spelt like that, no e's please, and not a hundred boys, biographers, there were forty-eight—this was the period when our tight little brotherhood really became a live thing. Stuart, the eldest, was away in the Army, 1914–18, and then in the U.S.A. until 1924, so he was a shadowy figure and remained so for many years. We three, however, made the adventurous two hundred mile school journey together, back and forth, six times a year and, going through the same experiences, in succession, felt a tremendous bond which became closest in the early 1920s when, under Wilfrid's aegis, we had two splendid holidays, first in the Isle of Man and then on the Clyde, at Rothesay. We had huge fun. And this by the way covers the period when Malcolm was supposed to be in blind, bandaged purdah! We sailed, swam, played golf and badminton, went to the cinemas and theatres, we even danced! I'm not prepared to believe that Malcolm didn't remember these days with considerable, if carefully concealed, tenderness. He certainly was neither blind nor a cripple. Long before the 1920s, however, the still cheery, still bad-tempered (though I can't remember what sort of thing used to upset him) infant of the trio was doing a line of his own, as a "memory man". He would suddenly embrace a topic, soak it up—and then pass on to something else. The unusual, but by no means unique, gift of the photographic memory—or total recall—was his. Malcolm's choice of subjects was odd—I remember, among others, hymns (with their tunes, titles, composers and

metres); golfballs—names, weights, sizes, floating or non-floating;
footpaths and tracks, distances to and from; gramophone records
(make, i.e. H.M.V., Decca, Parlophone etc., sung by, accompanied
by, band of, by, with, to or from). He also liked long words, at
which he had splendid bashes—he was, for instance, often
"dettermined", to rhyme with "letter signed". Or shorter, tricky
spellings/pronunciations, such as "mizzled", for misled. And his
rendering of a mishit tended to cause fraternal merriment. Among
his earliest favourite authors was one Talbot Baines Reed—(surely
he of the Fifth Form at St. Dominic's?)—Malcolm always called
him *Tablet* Baines Reed. It is a tiny but strange coincidence that
he was destined to be buried by a Rev. Talbot Baines. We all read
a lot. The picture of Inglewood as a cultural desert is overdone.
And Malcolm's more erudite tastes did not develop until much
later, by which time he had ample opportunity to satisfy them, if
so inclined.

Malcolm and I overlapped at two schools, unlike the others, and
we were both based on Inglewood for some years after Stuart
and Wilfrid had gone. Hence our particularly close relationship
during this period. Up to the age of about sixteen he conformed
to type as a hearty, hungry, laughing games-playing schoolboy.
He remained rather awkward and was completely unmechanical,
so, for instance, was in deep trouble if the chain came off his
bicycle. He was still very irritable and went fiery red in the face
when angry. He thus acquired the nickname Lobs, which has
mystified the biographers. It was simply short for Lobster. It was
never used in the family so he must have declared it, on the
Pyrrhus for instance, and it follows that he didn't mind being Lobs
for Lobster. With his awkwardness went a degree of accident-
proneness and a certain naïveté. All these things were rather endearing—and indeed he was a very endearing sort of person.
Always fun to be with, kind, generous, helpful—and as far as I
know he remained all these things, in his essential self.

At around sixteen he did certainly change from the conventional
schoolboy type. It would be odd not to change, with adolescence
—but he did it more radically than most. During an exchange of
correspondence several years ago Professor Bradbrook, author of
the only valid "life" so far, suggested that, feeling athletically
frustrated and overshadowed—presumably by the rest of us—
he took to the pen as a weapon against the world. I couldn't, and

still don't agree, because that situation simply didn't exist. None of us could even dream of emulating Wilfrid with his galaxy of caps and cups. If any of us had a success, everybody was tickled to bits. And in general the muscularity of the family has been wildly overworked. There was no pressure, no jealousy, no reason to feel frustrated or overshadowed. But the fact remains that Malcolm did start writing spirited, often caustic articles and reports in the *Leys Fortnightly*, the school magazine, and himself turned decidedly rebellious. He told me a story about a dreadful scene with, and a brutal beating by, a certain master with whom he had previously got along very well. The experience had turned him sour. Unfortunately Malcolm had become an inveterate liar, a fact which I have found very hard to swallow for he had at no time any reason to lie to me, or I to him. Not knowing quite when he took to lying I don't know whether to believe the beating story or not, and can only say that it seems more likely than athletic inadequacy as a turning point in his attitudes.

The articles in the *Fortnightly* were popular—at the Leys games were taken seriously while in progress, not afterwards. And if we were taught anything there, it was to enjoy a good leg-pull. Also to administer one. So he was taken along on a hockey trip to France, where he probably got drunk but managed to conceal it, and in due jollity acquired the nickname *"Ça Va"*. Before the expedition I had tried to hammer in a few phrases of useful as distinct from merely grammatically accurate French. This, the colloquial equivalent of "Fair enough" or "O.K." was the only one that stuck. And it stuck so fast that years later, when being married in Paris, it is on record that his answer to the central question was— *"Ça Va!"*

So in 1925 Malcolm's prosaic, humdrum way of life had done a hiccup both literally and symbolically. There had also been moves within the family which are significant in the ebb and flow of relationships. In this year Wilfrid married and left our immediate orbit. I myself was in France most of the time, but came home during academic vacations. Stuart had returned after five years in America—not as quite the roystering John Wayne figure depicted in some quarters, but our centre of gravity did move in his direction and we began to nibble at the bonds of parental authority which were increasingly irksome.

In 1926 I was back home, apprenticed to the family cotton

business. I had a motor bicycle and a few shillings, which meant that during Malcolm's vacations we could get around together far more easily than before, whether to golf (for a while—fading after the abortive "Championship") to still popular, widespread and amazingly cheap cinemas and music-halls or small boat racing in the Mersey. In the fullness of time, on Sunday mornings we tended to buy each other a pint of beer at the "Coach & Horses" in Greasby. We used to think this quite adventurous and I still find it impossible to believe that Malcolm was already an alcoholic within the accepted meaning of the term. The occasional "jag" maybe, but regular drinking would be impossible. He had neither the means, nor the opportunity. The booze of half a century ago, seen through—or in—today's glasses looks dirt cheap: whisky and gin at 12/6d (65 "new" pence) a bottle; beer a few coppers a pint. But money was scarce stuff. Very scarce. And there was no source of alcohol in Caldy, where we lived.

During this period the Ukelele (later dignified into a taropatch, whatever that may be) entered my life and hence Malcolm's. Having mastered "Swanee River", "Nearer My God to Thee", and a few others we moved on to "composing" atrocious doggerel ditties such as "I've Said Goodbye to Shanghai". We even did a double act at a charity concert. Just before our turn came on Malcolm told me he'd had rather a lot of beer to work up some courage. At that moment I wished I had too!

Still later we hawked the Shanghai thing, and an even worse one called "Marching down the High Road to China", around back-stage Liverpool. Eventually these were "published"—at father's expense be it said—and heard of no more. The incident is used in the *Volcano*. The prevalence of the oriental flavour in these deathless compositions is not, I think, connected at all with the *Pyrrhus* voyage. The 1920s had seen a succession of "China incidents" and these created topicality.

It is difficult, and not perhaps all that important, to pinpoint the exact sequence of events through this period, but they are years which I remember with special warmth. Malcolm and I saw less of each other than before, because we were in and out of the house at different times. But the days or weeks, or only evenings, we spent together were great fun. We were both grown men— or liked to think we were—and the world was before us, a remote, difficult world, but we'd cope all right and I don't think either of us doubted for a moment that our relationship would continue indefinitely. . . . Before the sailing of the *Pyrrhus* we'd looked up all the books we could find for hints and tips about nautical affairs. I gave him a clasp-knife as a parting gift, and he was off. Which brings me back to earth with a jolt.

In years to come Malcolm was to resent, bitterly, the publicity accompanying his departure. The family limousine, chauffeur-driven, at the dock-side. The "No silk cushions for me says wealthy cotton broker's son" headlines. But the publicity was laid on by Malcolm, who thoroughly enjoyed it. Not by father, who didn't. The apparent puzzle clears itself when we remember that at this time our bold hero regarded himself as a song-writer, to whom publicity was the breath of life. Not by any stretch of imagination did he regard himself as a famous novelist, or foresee that, reversing the poetic order of things, *Doctor* and *Saint* would eagerly frequent him, and hear great argument about him and about!

It was good to see him back after six months on the *Pyrrhus*. He had "filled out" to an extraordinary extent on hard manual work and (compared with the swill provided at school) good food, so he was no longer a boy but the hairy, barrel-chested man of many subsequent pictures. We spent long cheery hours over his adventures and evolved an early version of *Ultramarine*. This oddly enough was my suggestion for a title, an obvious pun, because he, still thinking of songs, wanted a Blues. Another was "Penalty Goal"—a much more involved pun around the facts that the *Pyrrhus* was a "goal-post" ship (so called from her layout of masts and derricks)—and that Malcolm had had a pretty rough time.

This seems an appropriate moment to say, firmly, that Malcolm had no "calling" at all for the sea, at this age—whatever he may have developed, or assumed, later. Nor did he ever hear any rollicking yarns about his grandfather Boden, because there weren't any, or see any relics or souvenirs, because there weren't any of those either, at least not according to a cousin who was born and grew up under the same roof as Grandma Boden. We'll leave it at that. The original germ of the desire to "rough it" was planted by a rather unpleasant youth at the Leys, son of a colonial pro-consul. It did not come from any romantic nautical association real or imaginary.

So there was a partial reversion to song-writing and strumming, but the *Pyrrhus* had made Malcolm miss the academic tide, which, turning in October, left him a year astern of station for getting up to Cambridge. Part of this year was spent in Bonn where he was supposed to learn some German. As with the French trip I tried to hammer in a few phrases. In vain, and the Gothic type still in use in those days was beyond his enthusiasm. He played his ukelele all day, and most of the night, while kind people poured wine into him. According to himself, but who is to believe what? Because some supervision did exist, he had sundry pals who, answering the cry *"Sind Sie im Bett Herr Lowry?"* would cry *"Jawohl Herr Doktor!"* and, satisfied that this rudimentary roll-call would be filled, Malcolm swam on into a haze of one of the world's most delectable products. But he didn't appreciate it, and he certainly learned no German, except perhaps *"Prosit"*, *"Gesundheit"* and *"Noch Ein!"*.

Malcolm was actually a poor linguist, which was a pity, because he had tremendous *Sprachgefühl* and an outstandingly good memory. He just couldn't be bothered learning those rules which have to be known before they can be forgotten, disregarded, or messed about with. Even if he had acquired these skeleton-keys to the Indo-European group of languages, they would not have admitted him to the impenetrable fastnesses of Scandinavia with which he pretended to be so familiar. My impression is that most of the linguistic embroidery so ably and emotively woven into his work consists of quotations from public notices, rules, regulations, advertisements and things of that kind, easily copied out, or in his case remembered. His apparent erudition should not be taken without the customary grain of salt. He did not work at any of his half dozen places of education and would not find many libraries in his future succession of flophouses and log-cabins. One does not become a scholar casually, or by mistake. But if and when he did come across an abstruse tome or complicated thought process which intrigued him, he'd suck it dry, remember it and insert it somewhere, probably upside down, in whatever pattern was occupying him.

We remained on good terms through his Cambridge days, but the ice was getting imperceptibly thinner beneath us. He swash-buckled his way through life while I, having become engaged to be married, presented a lower profile. He got drunker oftener, though I never ever did see him really tight. He would usually be home (last bus around 10 p.m.!) in time for a laugh in my room, which was next to his, at the far end of the corridor from the parental chamber. Inevitably there came an evening, probably in 1932, when he arrived with a heavier than usual load, and in one of his bad tempers. Aggressively drunk. I told him to hop it. The result was a most unseemly brawl. Nobody won but both were damaged. And though the house was in an uproar, nobody stirred and nothing was ever said. But that was the "end of a beautiful friendship". Not the fight itself, though that was a discreditable affair. We had simply run out of road.

It really is proving difficult to show the trends and influences fermenting in Malcolm's life without using specific incidents as punctuation marks. Sometimes the incidents don't fit into the accepted chronology. Such a one is the voyage to Norway, on a freighter, to find the poet Nordahl Grieg. This is another story which does not add up. We were both (Malcolm and I, not the poet) based on Inglewood that summer of 1930. Malcolm's birthday was 28 July, and the gloomy childhood incident is stark truth, not fiction, which torpedoes the July to September absence of the biographies. But even if the birthday dinner was in 1931—which is unlikely—I simply do not believe Malcolm was capable of finding himself a ship, in Preston, forty miles away, getting himself signed on as a fireman, disappearing into space for three months and then reappearing at home without anybody noticing! I do recall that he was away for a while. His own story at the time was that he had been up in Scotland where he had renewed a friendship with people we had met years before, on holiday, and had gone sailing with them in Clyde waters. We talked at length about the sailing, and the people. Why make up, for me, such a simple piece of gossip, if a slab of real life and excitement was there wanting to be told? If it is expedient to believe that he did go to Oslo, and did meet Nordahl Grieg, there is a much easier explanation of how it could be done. While in Scotland—not necessarily seeing our old friends—he had only to ring, or write to, father, sell him the story of an important poet whom he absolutely must see, and as soon as the fare came through he'd be on his way, from Leith, or Newcastle. He had already, the previous year sold a more preposterous yarn which got him to Cape Cod, and Conrad Aiken. Oslo would be a doddle, and this is the story I'd put my money on if—repeat if—we are convinced

21

that Malcolm really did meet the poet, a matter on which I have no views, except to point out that the evidence produced in support would make a cat laugh. A Cheshire cat, at that. The trampship from Preston, and its penultimate wanderings, I simply cannot swallow.[1]

It must be clear by now that Malcolm would have had no trouble at all making up the Grieg story from beginning to end, filling in the gaps with hardships and coincidences. Perhaps also a gramophone record from *die Niebelungen*! And in next to no time he would have convinced himself that it was all true. I should have more pity on the biographers.

The plain fact behind all these early travels (whether some of them happened or not!) is that father, although he didn't like spending money and in general allowed us all as little rope as he possibly could, was only too glad to get Malcolm out of the house. The bad temper, which in later years was to become on occasion homicidal, was already showing itself in bursts of violence both of language and behaviour towards his mother (who would be over sixty) and the dear old cook and housemaid who had been our lifelong friends. During weekdays in vacation time he was alone in the house with them.

In an attempt to appease him, and sensibly enough give him somewhere to spread out his papers and write or read, or play his (my actually, and I still have it) famous taropatch, a big quiet room at the top of the house was furnished as a study for him. No good. No booze. No amusing company. He seems to have found both among the Furness brothers—later sublimated into the Taskersons. Malcolm had known them at his first school, years earlier. I never met them. With the Furness brothers Malcolm did his marathon beerwalks and of course found Inglewood even more boring when he got back. Friction. Anger. Rage. Off goes the vicious circle. Initially Malcolm had no trouble "accounting for his movements" to father because Furness *père* was an eminent and highly respected Liverpool lawyer. It is strange that the "Furnace" family proved so difficult for certain people to trace. There are at least ten with and "e" in the telephone book, and at least another ten Furnisses, with an "i". No marks, Professors!

Malcolm's violence became a real nightmare to father. He was frightened to leave for his office in the morning: frightened what he might hear during the day or find in the evening. He was therefore glad to fall in with, and pay for, any wanderings, theoretically in search of culture, or experience, but in reality just to get shut of his wayward son for a while. Ultimately he would cause more and more trouble as he got further and further away, but that was still in the future.

When not being impossible Malcolm was his own cheery self, although he was steadily getting more bizarre, in his clothes, his behaviour and his general attitudes. Not to an extent which would raise an eyebrow now half a century later, but in the '30s he seemed decidedly eccentric. I think he did it partly for fun. He didn't give a damn, and had a great sense of whimsy. But partly, for sure, to put people off the scent. If nobody knew what he was going to say, or do, they wouldn't be surprised if he didn't! It got him into odd situations, which he enjoyed, and, oftener than not, it got him out again. It enabled him to dodge issues and disregard small details like the truth. Not with any evil intent necessarily, and never for gain, as such, since he never made any. Just for the hell of it. I remember him ringing once to say he'd be late home (so it must have been early days indeed). He'd met two very interesting chaps and was having a long important talk. It seemed an idea to ask who they were. A couple of names came back, but they happened to be a firm of local confectioners. I said so. He laughed, realizing who was on the line, and admitted he'd just read the names off a passing baker's van!

He moved on from minor duckings and weavings like this to less savoury fabrications. One that has a twist all of its own (because in this instance both sides were lying) is the story arising from a motor accident involving father and mother in 1942. It was quite a bad pile-up, and in a reproachful letter was laid at Malcolm's door on grounds of mental anguish caused by prodigal son and consequent reduction of concentration. In fact father wasn't driving. The chauffeur was. The mental anguish was genuine enough, but it wasn't sitting at the controls! And Malcolm's contrition is sheer eyewash, as witness the ham-and-tongue in cheek phraseology plus his own unaltered behaviour.

Another with a sour taste is the extraordinary yarn of Malcolm's utter horror when his adored elder brother Stuart was called upon by a cruel father to scale a church steeple, hard by the Inglewood grounds, and bring down the weathercock, in redemption of a long ago promise. The truth about this one concerns no steeple and no weathercock. Nor indeed is any such thing visible from Inglewood. The objects of the exercise were Liverpool's symbolic bronze deities, the Liver (to rhyme with diver) birds, each weighing many tons, perched on the domed turrets of the Liver Building from which neither Atlantic gales nor the fury of Hitler succeeded in moving them, let alone the earnest young Stuart who on "joining up" in 1914 jokingly undertook to "bring down one of those ruddy parrots for you"—or words to that effect—if he survived the war. The thing became a family joke and must have been well known to Malcolm. In any case the "confrontation"— if it happened—can not have been until 1924 when Stuart returned from America and Malcolm, by then fifteen, was surely beyond the nursery horrors stage.

Perhaps nastiest of all he didn't hesitate to suggest, after father's death, that this had been caused by cirrhosis of the liver through years of secret drinking, although he knew perfectly well that his father's whole lifetime intake of alcohol would not have served to open one morning eye for him, Malcolm. Apparently he just couldn't stop lying. Or didn't want to.

And yet, and yet, there is a little unpublished story called "Enter One in Sumptuous Armour", of which I have been able to glance through a photostat, and in which he describes with minute accuracy events belonging to his earliest days at the Leys, introduced by an equally exact impression of the trimestrial migration schoolwards and home again. There is, of course, embroidery. He plays at least two parts himself and has written me into alternative roles heavily disguised with a stammer and a Welsh accent. He seems to have worked on this piece from time to time and has blown think-balloons all over the place, rather spoiling both the theme and its legibility. My point is that he could, if he wanted, stick to a basically true story, and tell it well. Essential parts of this one were known only to him and to me, so there can be no question of mistaken identities. It just seems a pity that he couldn't stick to the facts a little oftener even if he put half the commentators out of business in the process!

Maybe I am too hard on the commentators who were certainly left with an enigma. To one of them at least I return thanks for the sentence "of his brother Russell he never spoke". Probably this was meant as a perfunctory dismissal of someone he couldn't be bothered to check out/up/on (according to taste). To me it came as a high tribute and further evidence that the essential Malcolm had not entirely decayed. He maligned and distorted everybody else because he probably hated himself for being beholden to them, and letting them down. So he hated them too. To understand Malcolm you must stand him on his head, and look at him sideways! He didn't have to hate me because our relationship was at an end. He valued it for what it had been—and shut up about it. I did the same, for twenty years or so.

If Malcolm could only have drunk a lot less, and enjoyed it a lot more, he might have come across a phenomenon in the making of wine called *pourriture noble*—splendid decay, noble rot— which, working through the fungus *Botrytis Cinerea*, produces out of the surplus sugar within very special grapes, during very special seasons, a wine-essence "tasting" of nothing in particular (Hovis in general) but making a man feel on a spoonful as if he were Johann Sebastian Bach composing an accompaniment to *Paradise Lost* having just defeated Isaac Newton in a scientific argument. Or, possibly, having written *Under the Volcano!* Take your choice.

There can be no doubt about Malcolm's physical and temperamental decay, but unfortunately it was far from noble. We shall have to look elsewhere for the qualities he put into his work and the abilities that enabled him to do so. The first that comes to mind was the first one to show, in childhood—his formidable memory for details which he would "bank" in separate accounts, as it were, until there were enough to bubble over into a stream of thought. Similarly he "banked" words, especially obscure or unusual words, a process he started very young. His joy was then boundless if he could find a use for some rare item in his collection. The applications of this idea can be extended almost indefinitely, to cover anything and everything from stars to snails, from A to Z. It was his most useful tool.

Next, perhaps was persistence—I nearly said patience, but nobody as irritable as Malcolm could be called "patient". Maybe I'm still wrong and "absorption" would be nearer the mark. Absorption which took no account of time, while he was playing with words. I only saw this process in its early stages, long before *furor scribendi* set in, but it is, to me, symbolized by the word "plangent" which Malcolm loved, but couldn't find anything to do, sorry, with: until that glorious freezing, foggy, February afternoon of wandering around dockside Birkenhead when he returned triumphant to announce that a tramcar's bell didn't say "Ting Ting", it said "Ylang Ylang", which was really, truly, beautifully plangent. Since Birkenhead had the first tramcar system ever, and I don't think ever replaced any rolling stock, he was probably right. At any rate, my laughter over the incident was probably an early symptom of our eventual break-up. He was completely "absorbed". My laughter was an offence.

To sum up this particular aspect, surely anyone so utterly dedicated to, and absorbed in, words as Malcolm must eventually become pretty good at using them—given one more thing. Time. And of time Malcolm had all there was, because he never had to sell so much as a semi-colon. His father might huff and his father might puff—which he did—but his father would always pay, as Malcolm well knew having bullied him into a position where he had no real alternative but to give way, again and again. So Malcolm could afford to spend ten years writing and rewriting one novel. Whether this was the perfectionism of a Henry Royce who, it was said, couldn't bear to see a new motor car leave his factory because there was always something he wanted to improve, I don't know. My suggestion would be that Malcolm simply liked writing, liked looking at and rearranging his beloved words, in the manner of—any collector. Is it not significant that when he failed to find a publisher—or rather while finding twelve publishers—he just went on writing the same book? The *Volcano* was supposed to grow into a trilogy. It must be permitted to wonder—when?

Another obvious question must be what effect a little stern economic necessity—applied early enough—might have had on Malcolm? I very much doubt if the answer would have been what we'd wish—that he would have written a string of masterpieces and today, under seventy and still writing, would bestride the literary world. With hindsight I cannot believe it, although the notion did seem to make sense once upon a time. No, Malcolm was hell-bent. Left to himself, deprived of the subventions, allowances, and rescue operations—acknowledged mainly with insults— which followed him around for most of his life, he would have got there sooner, without having time to explore the bowels of his own volcano. The world would thereby have been deprived of one great book, rather than gaining several.

In spite of all his meticulous mind-searchings, all his feats of memory-balancing in abstruse fields, all his perfectionism of rhythm, form and composition, Malcolm was never going to create anything, in the widest sense, beautiful. And goodness knows there is enough ugliness in the world already! But he lived, by choice, a squalid life, mainly in squalid circumstances. He was more interested in slime than in silk, in stinks rather than mere smells, in the sordid rather than the sublime. Granted, you can't have one without the other, all the time. He seemed to think he could—wrong way round. The boiling muck under his volcano was more appealing to him than the snow on its summit. He wallowed in one with no more than a passing glance at the other.

In spite of his ample sense of humour and his once cheerful personality the real essence of Malcolm's existence was *nostalgie de la Boue*. I shall never forget the glee with which he seized upon some lines of Geoffrey Chaucer as a prologue for his *Ultramarine*. They make an equally fitting epilogue to his whole life:

> Tak any brid, and put it in a cage,
> And do al thyn entente and thy corage
> To fostre it tendrely with mete and drinke,
> Of alle deyntees that thou canst bithinke,
> And keep it al-so clenly as thou may;
> Al-though his cage of gold be never so gay,
> Yet hath this brid, by twenty thousand fold,
> Lever in a forest, that is rude and cold,
> Gon ete wormes and swich wrecchednesse.

A sad little afterglow comes with this quotation. The volume was mine and I still have it. Leafing through to check the exact words I found the corner of the page still turned down to mark our discovery of this fragment from "The Maunciple's Tale" fifty years ago. But, after all, what is fifty years to Chaucer, with six centuries already behind him. And to Malcolm?

NOTES

1   A letter from Malcolm to Nordahl Grieg, dated 1938, speaks of correspondence and meeting seven years earlier (*Selected Letters*, 1967, p. 15)—(editor's note).

1

Under the Volcano—The Way it Was: A Thirty-Year Perspective

by RICHARD HAUER COSTA

Towards the end of his posthumously published novella *The Forest Path to the Spring*, Malcolm Lowry rages against giving in to the Consul's *angst*, the tyranny of the past:

> It was my duty to transcend [the past] in the present . . . Sometimes I had the feeling I was attacking the past rationally as with a clawbar and hammer, while trying to make it into something else for a supernatural end. In a manner I changed it by changing myself and having changed it found it necessary to pass beyond the pride I felt in my accomplishment, and to accept myself as a fool again.[1]

The persona here is recording something closely akin to Thoreau's experience at Walden Pond (". . . the significance of the experience lay not in the path at all, but in the possibility that in converting the very cannister I carried . . . to use I had prefigured something I should have done with my soul. . . ."). The speaker, as every Lowrian knows, is seeing the sylvan as symbolic; he wears a mask of bucolic rebirth. Viewing his jazz-musician's life as a shipwreck ("I must have stumbled into a thousand alcoholic dawns"), he knows he must transcend the hubris that has driven him to read messianic portents in every passing moment; must return to a state where he is innocent of such perceptions.

This Dostoevskian notion that a return to innocence can emerge, Phoenix-like, from the ashes of excess makes *Forest Path* the most hopeful of Lowry's writings. Although return-to-innocence didn't work—sobriety didn't happen—for Lowry as artist or man, it strikes me as providing a chastening directive for my pursuance of this assignment in Anne Smith's book. I cannot view *Under*

29

the Volcano from a thirty-year perspective without trying to return to *the way it was* before this once-subterranean book became an industry. To one who read *Under the Volcano* and fell forever under its spell within a few days of its original publication in February of 1947, it has not been as breathtaking as one might have assumed to have watched—eventually participated—the takeover of the book by academic specialists: the equivalent of what R. P. Blackmur, writing of *Ulysses*, called "the whole clutter of exegesis, adulation, and diatribe".[2]

2

Today it is simply not possible to *discover* a new book the way one could thirty years ago. To do so requires freedom from the New York-based media gristmill which merchandises even bad books into best-sellerdom months before publication. To do so requires ignorance of an author's previous books and of his/her name itself. In North America, at least, Malcolm Lowry and *Under the Volcano* met all the terms. His only previous book, *Ultramarine*, had been published fourteen years before and only in his native England. The name could only have been known to me if I'd read more regularly than I did Whit Burnett's *Story*, which published two Lowry fictions in the early 1930s.[3] Yet it would be fatuous of me to pretend that I bought the novel while brousing in a bookstore. Two forces brought the book to my attention: a professor's enthusiasm and an unforgettable review.

Leonard Brown was a legendary and, by his own choice, an un-Ph.D-ed professor whose students at Syracuse University had included Shirley Jackson and Stanley Edgar Hyman. I was studying journalism, not literature, but any word from Brown tended to be passed along. Brown, almost a commuter to and from Mexico, announced to his students that winter of '47 that he had just read a book having a Mexican setting and by a new writer, Malcolm Lowry—a work he believed without qualm to be the most important novel in English since *Ulysses*. A more direct prompting to action was provided by John Woodburn's cover review in the *Saturday Review of Literature* (10 February 1947). These were the latter days of that publication before it dropped "of Literature" from its name; while it was still concerned for literature rather than forced into the care and feeding of *kitsch*. Near the close of that review, long portions of which I committed to memory, Woodburn wrote:

> I have never before used the word in a review, and I am aware of the responsibility upon me in using it, but I am of the opinion, carefully considered, that *Under the Volcano* is a work of genius.

It is no longer possible to recall what in the book caught me up from the first word, sped me through it in a single sitting, and prompted me for the only time in my life to begin it again immediately. I can only say that the opening chapter, considered in terms of conventional fiction all wrong—an epilogue in the place of a prologue; an opening in which the fate of the two main characters is revealed; a chapter which is itself a series of intricate flashbacks and where Mexican local colour, as an unsympathetic reader for Jonathan Cape put it, is "heaped on in shovelfuls"—struck me as *right*. If the opening chapter denies the suspense of *impending* catastrophe, Lowry provides something equally dramatic and more consonant with the mood of the book: a sense of dread at what has *already* occurred, a thing so shattering that it has left the survivors no peace during the intervening year.

In those first readings—in *all* subsequent ones—it never occurred to me to ask such interlocking questions as why the Consul drinks or why, given the kind of desperate love for his wife Yvonne that his unsent letter reveals (in itself an entire love-sonnet sequence in prose), the Consul rejects her throughout the long day of her return.

If it is not quite true to say that Geoffrey Firmin is like Gulley Jimson, a character who should not be judged but enjoyed, he is without doubt truly tragic in at least one classic sense: his stature is to be judged by the extent of his fall. That fall is not only verified by the first chapter, an overture in the form of an elegy. It looms irrevocably from the start of the action proper, in Chapter II, when the returning Yvonne, having arrived by taxi outside the Bella Vista bar, enters at seven in the morning of the Day of the Dead only to see the man she has divorced but still loves making a supreme effort to build himself to his feet.

The reunion scene—a drunkard's tableau—never really changes. Lowry uses dipsomania to give the appearance of diffused attention, the Consul's professed aspirations, like himself, always tottering. But even an initial reading, if intense, affirms the futility of what

Dale Edmonds brilliantly, if ironically, labels the book's "salvage operations".[4] The Consul, with Bartleby, with the Underground Man, with Meursault, never doubts where his preferred destination lies. He simply chooses *not* to—not to act, not to alter his course for love, not to save himself. Human options pale beside the Consul's "battle for the survival of consciousness", which is another way of saying his imperative for preserving his own identity, however harmful to himself are the means. The Consul knows the world, and he opts out of it—the Consular equivalent of the Underground Man's most advantageous advantage.

Of course, in the manner of Jake Barnes in *The Sun Also Rises* (a book at one in tone with *Under the Volcano* although its opposite in weave and texture), Geoffrey dare not banish illusion of recovery ("Isn't it pretty to think so?" Jake, in desolate cajolery, tells Brett in the last line of the novel.). The Consul hovers at times between a seemingly attainable paradise and a desperately sought *barranca*. Lowry's major triumph in *Under the Volcano* lies in his making forceful the attempts of the other four principals (Dr. Vigil ought not to be overlooked here) to save the Consul while making inevitable the Consul's rejection of those attempts. The Consul, in fact, may be the first character in fiction to reflect fully the *noblesse oblige* of the addict, the kind of pride that must be asserted to seek in drink a means of transcending the agony of consciousness. He is the supreme exemplar in modern fiction of self-knowledge that makes action an affront to self.

Stephen Spender was the first to warn that if the disintegration of the Consul as an alcoholic "takes over" the novel cannot succeed.[5] It is the artistic problem of the novel to make the Consul stand for *more* than a justification—or even, an apology—for the lot of the addict, more than a figment of extended autobiography. The Consul ought not, if the novel is to prosper on its highest plane, be his own special case. For me, Lowry avoids the "clinical" fallacy by treating Geoffrey's alcoholism as a kind of tragic game with overtones of high comedy. He achieves in his portrayal of the Consul's mescal-soaked consciousness a deftly patterned—wild but never improbable—medley of memories, free fancies, conversational snatches, absurdities, improvisations. Lowry maintains a maelstrom harmony between the physical world of the Consul—the demonic—and the fantasy-harbour where deliverance might lie. As evolved by Lowry over nearly a decade of reworkings—determinedly sober and extraordinarily controlled reworkings—*Volcano* pays off on both upper and lower storeys: the fall of a man of sensibility who is also subject to the earthly disasters of the addict.

3

When *Under the Volcano* was published in 1947, the world was still digging out of the ruins of the Second World War. However, Lowry wrote the crucial draft in Mexico during the war's prelude period; the loss of the Battle of the Ebro in the Spanish Civil War is a recurring reference. The main dialectic of the novel is a debate between Geoffrey and his half-brother Hugh in Chapter X on the futility of involvement (the Consul's view) in all those "people's revolutions", including the war in Spain, that were so much a part of the political climate when Lowry began the book. These years—1936–38—were times when ominous notes of exile and doom were being sounded in the works of novelists as little known as Louis-Ferdinand Céline and as successful as Erich Maria Remarque. However, neither the malaise of alienation nor the Bartlebyan prerogative that was to carry the name "existentialism" was yet large enough a subject, except in France, for other than melodramatic treatment in, say, the "entertainments" of Graham Greene and the tough crime stories of Dashiell Hammett and Raymond Chandler.

When Lowry's Consul emerged, he was passed over entirely in Britain and damned by the pseudo-literary praise of the Luce press in the United States. *Time*'s accolade may have intimidated the *New Yorker* into dismissing the book in a paragraph as being "a rather good imitation of an important novel" (that magazine apparently recanted fifteen years later when, in a review of the first U.S. edition of *Ultramarine*, it referred to *Volcano* as a "truly great novel").[6] Not even *Time* could shake the general reader from the notion that Geoffrey Firmin was more than an already out-of-vogue kinsman of Don Birnam, the drunken hero of Charles Jackson's *Lost Weekend*, published three years before. It is unlikely, despite Lowry's often expressed feeling that the earlier book spoiled the psychological moment for his own, that the mass of readers who made a best-seller of an alcoholic's monumental binge on Third Avenue would (or could) do much with a drunken, disgraced British ex-consul staggering through the streets of a seedy

Mexican town, called Quauhnahuac, quoting Dante and Marlows. The "first" book (and for the record, Lowry's composition of the early drafts of *Volcano* preceded Jackson by at least five years) made a peripety of a Jewish holiday, which kept pawnshops closed and Birnam sober; *Under the Volcano* made the Mexican Day of the Dead an archetypal holiday standing for Humanity's last gasp. For, as Hugh Firmin puts it while discussing with Yvonne the problem of the man's drinking: "What's the good? Just sobering him up for a day or two's not going to help. Good God, if our civilization were to sober up for a couple of days it'd die of remorse on the third."[7]

The earliest "review" of *Volcano* was never published. It was a disheartening report from Jonathan Cape late in 1945 calling for major cuts and revisions as a condition of acceptance. Although the critique is mentioned in Lowry studies only because it evoked a thirty-page epistolary rebuttal which Spender has declared ought to become a standard preface to the novel, the demurrers portend the sense of later criticism. The reader (only lately identified from his posthumous autobiography as the highly respected William Plomer) objects to the very things supporters find extraordinary: the *longueurs*—the mood music—of a lush style by which, in Plomer's words, Lowry presents "flashbacks of the characters' past lives and past and present thoughts and emotions . . . Mexican local colour heaped on in shovelfuls . . . the mescal-inspired phantasmagoria, or heebie-jeebies, to which Geoffrey has succumbed".[8] Only the handling of local colour wins Plomer's unqualified admiration; the "feel" of drunkenness as simultaneously self-defeating and a buffer, as Lowry later put it, "against the baffling sterility of life as it is sold to you" is lost on Plomer who finds these sections "too long, wayward, and elaborate" and, unkindest cut of all to Lowry, suggestive of *Lost Weekend*.

Today, as Douglas Day observes, the report no longer strikes one as startling.[9] I have written elsewhere of the shock-of-recognition I felt when I first read an account of how, in 1912, the French publisher Fasquelle assigned Proust's 712-page typescript of the *Recherche* to his reader, the poet Jacques Madeleine.[10] The pejoratives of the Fasquelle and Cape policemen provide a study in the echolalia of critics. Madeleine writes that "the whole of this first part [says Proust] is merely 'a preparation', a 'poetic overture'. . . . This 'preparation' does not prepare anything; it

gives no inkling of what . . . is to follow. . . ." Cape's reader
accuses Lowry of perpetrating "a gamey and outworn trick to
begin at the end of the book" and excoriates him for "flashbacks
of the characters' past lives and past and present thoughts and
emotions [that are] often tedious and unconvincing". The judgment of time has taken good care of such charges as M. Madeleine's that Proust requires seventeen pages—including one sentence of forty-four lines—to describe the remembered difficulties
of a small boy getting to sleep.

Such books either excite readers, or they do not. Plomer's report
merits respect for it pointed early and effectively to the recurrent
theme of most of the adverse criticism of Under the Volcano
these thirty years: the excess of its virtues. Of the first major
reviews in the U.S., almost all of which were largely favourable,
only the aforementioned by Woodburn and Mark Schorer's in
the New York Herald Tribune refrain from qualifying their praise
with warnings about stylistic excesses. Jacques Barzun's review in
Harper's (May 1947) was the least responsible of the early assess-
ments. It elaborated the New Yorker's squib about Volcano's being
an imitation of an important novel and charged Lowry with
having written "a long regurgitation of the materials found in
Ulysses" and "while imitating the tricks of Joyce, Dos Passos and
Sterne [given] us the heart and mind of Sir Philip Gibbs". Professor Barzun had just begun what was to be a long stint of
reviewing with Harper's, and the space available to him was admit-
tedly small. And, to be honest about it, how could he know that
the question of influence was to be so thorny a one with Lowry?
However, as Lowry himself put it in his able and predictable response, he had never read Ulysses through and was only casually
acquainted with the other "materials" Barzun cites as creditors.

Barzun's strategy is that of the name-dropper who hits-and-
runs. He accuses Lowry of being derivative and lets it go at that.
Many subsequent studies have elaborated Lowry's indebtedness to
Joyce without suggesting specific parallels. My own theory, which
I still hold although I first aired it a decade ago, is that Lowry
learned whatever he needed to know about Ulysses through his
acknowledged symbiosis with Conrad Aiken who, in turn, has
spoken of the first appearance of Ulysses in 1922 as a turning-
point in his own developing aesthetic of the novel.[11]

The first reviews that were not written against the stringent deadlines and space limitations of the dailies and weeklies were those by R. W. Flint in *Kenyon Review* (summer 1947) and Robert B. Heilman in *Sewanee Review* (summer 1947). As if by design, these two reviews defined the readability dialectic that still, after thirty years and all the encomiums of "contemporary classic" and "the last masterpiece", makes *Under the Volcano* a much-discussed but little-read book.

Whatever praise Flint can muster has to be backed into. "In the matter of style, Mr. Lowry is energetic but no Thomas Wolfe. . . . All of the book, the lyrics bursts, the journalese, the midway of styles and verbal games, labours under a burden of irony that is a token of the author's failure to save himself from spiritual vulgarity and achieve authentic tragic insight. . . . Each of his characters is only part of the modern tragic personality, caught between meaningless absolutes, that Mr. Lowry has not quite courage enough to represent. . . ." Mr. Flint's favourite word is "authentic". It becomes one of those "meaningless absolutes" to which he refers. My guess is that he made it only as far as the first pages of Chapter II where one learns that the Consul has no socks on, a detail that enables Flint to infer, not a drunk's dishevelment, but his degradation as a British subject. Although the review drones off in arch scapegoatism in which he makes the book pay for his own biases, Flint is the first to praise the book on a basis that would prevent Lowry from voicing one complaint Joyce made of the early critics of *Ulysses*: "They might at least have said it was damned funny." Flint on *Volcano*: "The humor may be the most authentic part of the book."

Heilman, given exactly the same space as Flint—four pages— meets the novel on its terms ("The nexuses are imaginative rather than casual, or logical, or chronological; hiatuses compel a high attention; dextrous leaps are called for. In such a sense *Under the Volcano* may be understood as poetic. . . ."). He is the first to understand—and say in a review—that what Joseph Frank said of Joyce ("The reader is forced to read *Ulysses* in exactly the same manner as he reads poetry—continually fitting fragments together and keeping allusions in mind until, by reflexive reference, he can link them to their complement") can be said of the author of *Volcano*. Heilman's review opens up the book, and no reading since touches more cogently, in so little space, the Lowryan promissory notes that are paid in full at the end.

So, besides reading the story as story, we are always aware of a multitude of suggestions which, in their continual impingement upon us, remind us of the recurrent images of Shakespeare. The action takes place in November, on the Day of the Dead; Geoffrey feels his "soul dying"; a funeral takes place; burial customs, the shipping of a corpse are discussed; an earlier child of Yvonne's is dead; Geoffrey thinks he is seeing a dead man; a cantina is called La Sepultura; Geoffrey's recalls Dr. Faustus's death; a dead dog is seen in a ravine; a dying Indian is found by the roadside. Always there are vultures, pariah dogs, the noise of target practice. There are a decaying hotel, a reference to the House of Usher, the ruins of the palace of Maximilian and Carlotta. Geoffrey's soul appears to him "a town ravaged and stricken"; an imaginary "little town by the sea" burns up. Frustrations and failures are everywhere—engagements are missed, the light fails in a cinema. Always we are reminded of the barranca, or ravine, near the town—a horrendous abyss. Once it is called "Malebolge"; there are various allusions to Dante's *Inferno*; Geoffrey feels he is in hell, quotes Donne on sin, looks at Cocteau's *La Machine Infernale*, takes a ride in a Maquina Infernal; calls ironically-defiantly, "I love hell"; at the end he is in a bar "under the volcano." "It was not for nothing the ancients had placed Tartarus under Mt. Aetna. . . ." There are continual references to Marlowe's Faustus, who could not pray for grace, just as Geoffrey cannot feel a love that might break his love for alcohol, or rather, symbolize a saving attitude; as in the Faustus play, *soul* is a recurrent word. There is an Eden-Paradise theme; a public sign becomes a motif in itself, being repeated at the end of the story: "Do you enjoy this garden, which is yours? Keep your children from destroying it!" Geoffrey's own garden, once beautiful, has become a jungle; he hides bottles in the shrubbery; and once he sees a snake there.[12]

Having seen so much so quickly—and the above summary takes into account most of the territorial claims that were to be staked out over the next thirty years—Professor Heilman is too balanced a critic not to recognize the perils of excess:

> Mr. Lowry has an immensely rich and various imagination, and he never corks his cornucopia of evocative images and symbols. Some disciplinary rejections, some diffidence in setting afloat upon the imagination every boat that he finds upon the shore, would reduce the distractedness to which the reader is occasionally liable and would thus concentrate and shape the author's effect more clearly.

Heilman concludes his astounding review with the view, slightly qualified, that Malcolm Lowry has given the world a book that is keyed to the contemporary rhythm: "Such a multivalued poetic fiction . . . is *apparently* the especial labour of the artistic conscience at our turn of an epoch" (italics mine).

Writing just twenty years later, on the occasion of the publication of Lowry's *Selected Letters*, Christine Brooke-Rose concluded that they show "an astounding ignorance of what was really going on in literature".[13] Stephen Spender, writing about the same time, is willing to leave the matter ambiguous:

> Lowry has borrowed from Joyce, turned his symbolic devices upside down and used them for his own purposes either with audacious intelligence, or else from a kind of inspired misunderstanding.[14]

Lowry, himself, had no illusions about his ability to keep up. His alterego (Sigbjørn Wilderness) in the most autobiographical of his stories reports trying heroically, a few pages each night, to read Empson's *Seven Types of Ambiguity* while yearning for Aiken's *House of Dust*, the only literary work he has ever enjoyed with aesthetic detachment. He is

> capable of conceiving of a writer today, even intrinsically a first-rate writer who *simply cannot understand*, and never has been able to understand, what his fellow writers are driving at, and have been driving at, and who has always been too shy to ask.[15]

4

Two interlocking factors, I believe, were responsible for a fifteen-year delay in the onset of the Lowry industry. Although born in the Wirral country around Liverpool and educated at the Leys School and at Cambridge, Lowry never developed either an English identity or reputation. And, as a writer, he never had a second act.

I was less annoyed than amused when my publisher made it a condition of my contract that I write the Lowry book under a "Canadian Authors" imprint. Canada, in a sense, has a right to a proprietary interest. Mexico, too. He did all of his important creative work (1936–54) at the extremes of the North American continent. He lived a variation of the plot, and wrote the first

version, of *Under the Volcano* in Mexico, the country that his root-
less and self-destructive side saw, as one of his poems has it, as
"pyre of Bierce and springboard of Hart Crane".[16] He wrote these
additional versions, including the published one, of *Volcano*, the
revealing stories of *Hear Us O Lord*, and four unfinished novels,
two of which were published after his death, in Canada. No wonder
he asked readers to consider

> the plight of an Englishman who is a Scotchman who is a Nor-
> wegian who is a Canadian who is a Negro at heart from Dahomey
> who is married to an American who is on a French ship in dis-
> tress which has been built by Americans and who finds at last
> that he is a Mexican dreaming of the White Cliffs of Dover.[17]

I once heard Edmund Wilson tell a class of mine that it was a
disarming fact to him that so many American writers of his gener-
ation either wrote themselves out or lived themselves out before
they were forty—Fitzgerald, Wolfe, Hemingway, Hart Crane. He
had just turned seventy, was writing or revising three books, and
could not make us believe that his dismay was not mixed with
satisfaction over his own survivability. Lowry had no second act.
Under the Volcano became for fifteen years a subterranean work
—one that could not be kept in print—because there was no
follow-up that would send readers back to the one they had missed.

When Lowry died unexpectedly in the Sussex village of Ripe in
June of 1957, in his forty-eighth year, that death followed the
temporary fate of the book—remained unreported in the world
press for days, an underground thing, an unguarded secret, "death
by misadventure". "Malc dead suddenly," Margerie cabled his
friend, the novelist David Markson. But, somehow more surprising, the legacy, *Under the Volcano*, had been dead longer—out of
print for years.

Interest in Malcolm Lowry from his death until the publication
of the first of four posthumous books in 1961 was kept alive by
his widow Margerie, his close Canadian friend, the poet Earle
Birney, and special issues of *Canadian Literature*, which, under
George Woodcock's editorship, published in four supplements a
bibliography of works by and about Malcolm Lowry, edited by
Birney with the assistance of Mrs. Lowry.[18]

The first groundswell of interest in Lowry and *Volcano* from
Britain dates from this period. Philip Toynbee (the *Observer*, 29

April 1962), one of the many *literati* who missed the book first time round, atoned: "I am now persuaded Lowry was a great writer, and that *Under the Volcano* is one of the great English novels of this century." The same month, the leader in the *Times Literary Supplement* (Toynbee again?) describes *Volcano* as comparable to *Ulysses* "and for more poetic"—a classic. John Wain picks up the refrain a bit later, with characteristic ambiguity: "To me, *Ulysses* is a great book that almost didn't come off. *Under the Volcano* is a great book that almost did."[19] Walter Allen calls the novel the finest by an Englishman in the 1940s.[20] Anthony Burgess finds the Consul suggestive of the Promethean Rebel, a towering extension of Aiken's "Prufrock figures" which spawned him.[21] M. C. Bradbrook's *Malcolm Lowry: His Art and Early Life* (1974) is the first book, including Day's biography, to show from an English viewpoint, the importance of the Wirral to Lowry.

In the United States, *Prairie Schooner* becomes the first American literary journal to devote a whole issue to Lowry and *Volcano*.[22] Conrad Knickerbocker, a *New York Times* critic and apostle of the possessed and demonic, announces that he will write the authorized biography of Malcolm Lowry, but dies by his own hand in April 1966, aged thirty-seven, not long after returning from London where he interviewed, among many, Lowry's Cambridge contemporary, the critic John Davenport. Knickerbocker's work-in-progress is taken over by a University of Virginia Comparative Literature professor, Douglas Day, who will require seven years to get "this albatross of a book off my back"[23] but will win the 1974 National Book award for biography for his efforts.

Day's book, despite faults, is admirable, the most important single entry in the Lowry sweepstakes. He has given us a book which not only corrects previous biographical errors, including mine, but establishes firm out-of-bounds markers within which those cultists who would have us believe that only excess generates art will have to operate. If Day's study has a certain defect of its virtues—if it leaves unanswered the question of how Malcolm Lowry whose demonic life he so faithfully chronicled could produce an *Under the Volcano*—perhaps it is unfair to expect a biographer to record what may be unrecordable.

How a writer who normally could write about nothing but himself came to transcend the neuroses of his life and for once—it would never happen again—elevate the private to the Promethean is a progress that is not conveyed in even so superb a report. The clues to that progress, which was literary, not clinical, are buried in the labyrinth of *Under the Volcano*'s manuscripts at the University of British Columbia. Lowry's manner of composition, combining false starts exhaustively pursued and digressions and *longueurs* ruinously indulged, became a nightmare for a writer whose span would be predictably brief. But for a time—the final several years of the ten he needed to complete the book—Lowry's struggle was as directive as a sculptor's and as strategic as a film cutter's.

We get in Day's 483-page book only two pages (pp. 298–9) dealing with that temporary order in the fisherman's cottage at Dollarton, British Columbia, that produced the fourth and final version of *Volcano*. And it is that masterwork which will stand forever as a disclaimer to the life of addiction this biographer so painstakingly documents. Put another way, while it is true that no one but Malcolm Lowry could have created the Consul—a possessed man writing about a possessed man—it is also true that the Consul stands for more than the tragic-comic endomorph who died an alcoholic's death.

Day's analysis of *Under the Volcano* occupies some twenty-five pages.[24] Although he is contemptuous of nearly all previously published readings of the whole novel, his own contributes little that is new. He acknowledges frequently Dale Edmonds' justly praised "Reading of the Immediate Level" and adds five levels of his own: (1) Earthbound—the chthonic—in which he effectively describes Lowry's extraordinary Mexican tableau which no contemporary writer, except possibly Durrell with Alexandria, can match for *surreal* validity. With Lowry's Mexican interior, landscape and mindscape are one, a unity that a number of commentators have demonstrated though none so ably as the novelist William Gass. (2) Human: Day demonstrates how Lowry, a writer never before and never again able to create a character who was not a painful extension of himself, this time jumped over his shadow. (3) Political: the Consul, unimportant, even innocent, politically, is slain by Mexican Fascists for the ironic reason that he cannot, *in extremis*, properly identify himself as unimportant and innocent. (4) Magical: Day stays afloat where a number of prior commentators have drowned in the Cabalistic undertow.

It is only on the fifth level—the religious—that Douglas Day

THE ART OF MALCOLM LOWRY

stakes out a special claim. *Under the Volcano* is, he believes, "the greatest religious novel of this century" (p. 350). The key metaphysical marker, among so many, is the inscription which the Consul reads on the wall of the house of Jacques Laruelle, the French ex-film director who has been his wife's lover: *No se puede vivir sin amar.* For Day, the ultimate meaning of Fray Luís de Léon's words is this: without loving God, one cannot live eternally. The Consul's long day's dying, then, merely affirmed by his murder what the novel had fore- (and after-) shadowed from the start: without *agape*, love of one's fellow man, hell is in each man who is in bondage, like the Consul, to the provincialism of self.

Day thus extends a sense of the novel that Robert Heilman had first noted twenty-five years earlier.[25] He found Lowry's allusions —Dante, Faustus—so powerful as to propel the imagination beyond a historical present. Lowry's Christian echoes are decidedly ironic. In Chapter V, the Consul, in his rundown garden and in his cups, offers to his neighbour Quincey the possibility of Adam as the first property owner and God, the first agrarian, an analogue, he says, of the Marxist president of Mexico, Cárdenas. "But," for Heilman, "Lowry's whole complex of image and symbol is such as to direct a dissolving order, in search of a creative affirmation, toward that union of the personal and the universal which is the religious."

5

David Markson is a fifty-year-old American novelist who knew Lowry well though briefly in the early 1950s. It was at Markson's apartment in New York that Malcolm and Margerie stayed for a few days in 1954 just prior to their final departure from North America for Italy en route to England. Much later Markson wrote an imperishable memoir of Lowry during those last days, a man he never saw sober but about whom he is in agreement with that anonymous voice in a bar which once said, of Lowry, "The very sight of that old bastard makes me happy for five days. No bloody fooling."[26]

Markson, who struck up a correspondence with Lowry while writing his M.A. thesis on *Under the Volcano* (Columbia University, 1952) and was the recipient of as illuminating a series of letters as was ever written by an artist to a student, attends the Lowry sessions of the Modern Language Association whenever they are in New York. Dutifully listening while academic Lowrians chipped away at the rock with their Dantean motifs, Faustian archetypes, and Edenic echoes finally got to him. Recently he dispatched a 300-page typescript to a University Press at the other end of the country. Over the years the chipping away had many times drawn suspiciously close to his own thesis, which has always been standard reading for graduate students working on Lowry. So he expanded, fourfold, his old M.A. paper and deepened it. It took him, off and on, two years.

I have been fortunate in this thirtieth year of my perspective on *Under the Volcano* to have read Markson's book in manuscript. I am happy to be able to report that it was scheduled for publication late this year (1977), after unanimously favourable readers' reports. It is the definitive exegetical study, doing for student readers of *Volcano* what Harry Blamires' guidebook does for *Ulysses*. Its publication may even cut down the capers of lesser exegetes who, along with the cultists, have taken over the book.[27]

Also in the realm of salutary volcanic developments comes word that the work of Lowry scholars and archivists at the University of British Columbia goes on. W. H. New, who has been working for years to bring the secondary bibliography, started by Earle Birney, up to date, writes me that he is almost finished. Regretfully, I have lost touch with another U.B.C. scholar, Vik Doyen, since he left Canada to return to his native Belgium. Last I heard, he had completed a year bringing order to the many versions of *Under the Volcano*, from the "lost" Mexican manuscript of 1936–38 to the final one: a ten-year palimpsestic orgy which, given Lowry's method of composition, rivals the layers of history at Pompeii.

NOTES

1 Malcolm Lowry, "The Forest Path to the Spring", in *Hear Us O Lord From Heaven Thy Dwelling Place* (Philadelphia and New York, 1961), pp. 279–80.

2 R. P. Blackmur, "The Jew in Search of a Son", *Eleven Essays in the European Novel* (New York, 1964), p. 27.

3 Malcolm Lowry, "On Board the *West Hardaway*", *Story* III, 15 (October

1933), 12–22, and "Hotel Room in Chartres", *Story* V, 26 (September 1934), 53–8.

4 Dale Edmonds, *"Under the Volcano:* A Reading of the 'Immediate Level' ", *Tulane Studies in English* XVI (1968), p. 65.

5 Stephen Spender, Introduction, *Under the Volcano* (Philadelphia and New York, 1965), p. viii.

6 Both notices in the *New Yorker* were unsigned. The first appeared on 22 February 1947, p. 149. The second appeared on 13 December 1961, p. 125.

7 Malcolm Lowry, *Under the Volcano* (New York, 1947), p. 117. All references to the text of *Volcano* are to the 1947 Reynal & Hitchcock edition and are noted by page number in brackets.

8 *Selected Letters of Malcolm Lowry*, eds. Harvey Breit and Margerie Bonner Lowry (Philadelphia and New York, 1965), p. 61. The first I knew that William Plomer was the Jonathan Cape reader was when I read a review of *The Autobiography of William Plomer* by Alan Bell ("A Sense of Placeness", *Times Literary Supplement*, 10 October 1975, p. 1185): "Plomer's anger at the proposed publication of his report on Malcolm Lowry's *The Volcano*, which had occasioned a massive rejoinder from the author, is mentioned to show his high view of the privacy of such transactions."

9 Douglas Day, *Malcolm Lowry: A Biography* (New York, 1973), p. 316.

10 Richard Hauer Costa, "Lowry's Overture as Elegy", *A Malcolm Lowry Catalogue* (New York, 1968), pp. 41–3.

11 "*Ulysses*, Lowry's *Volcano*, and the *Voyage* Between: A Study of an Unacknowledged Literary Kinship", *University of Toronto Quarterly* XXXVI, 4 (July 1967), 335–52. My view of the Lowry-Aiken-Joyce "transfusion" is elaborated in slightly different form in my book. *Malcolm Lowry* (New York, 1972), pp. 26–44, and in my two brief memoirs of Conrad Aiken, "Lowry/Aiken Symbiosis", *Nation* CCIV, 26 26 June 1967), 823–6, and "Conrad Aiken (1889–1973): The Wages of Neglect", *Fiction International*, Nos. 2/3 (1974), 76–80.

12 Robert B. Heilman, a review in *Sewanee Review* LV (July-September 1947), 489–90. Professor Heilman extended this earliest and most favourable of the *Volcano* reviews in American quarterlies in 'The Possessed Artist and the Ailing Soul", *Canadian Literature No. 8* (Spring 1961), 7–16. That essay, *sine qua non* for students of *Under the Volcano*, has been reissued in *Malcolm Lowry: The Man and His Work*, ed. George Woodcock (Vancouver, 1971), pp. 16–25.

13 Christine Brooke-Rose, "Mescalusions", *London Magazine* (April 1967), p. 103.

14 Spender, Introduction, *op. cit.*, p. xiii.

15 Malcolm Lowry, "Through the Panama", in *Hear Us O Lord From Heaven Thy Dwelling Place* (Philadelphia and New York, 1961), p. 84.

16 Malcolm Lowry, "For *Under the Volcano*", *Selected Poems of Malcolm Lowry* (San Francisco, 1962), p. 24.

17 Lowry, "Through the Panama", *op. cit.*, p. 96.

18 This exhaustive compilation appears in *Canadian Literature:* Issues 8

(Spring 1961, 80–88); 9 (Summer 1961, 80–84); 11 (Winter 1962, 90–95); 19 (Winter 1964, 83–9). The bibliography is especially useful for its location of periodicals in which Lowry's posthumous poetry has appeared. Earle Birney writes: "Although it is fairly complete in respect to Malcolm Lowry's own writings . . . , it is incomplete in respect to published comment on his work and life." The accelerated interest in Lowry over the last fifteen years, as indicated and spurred by a spate of posthumous publications, justifies the full supplement to Birney's bibliography which is being completed, as this is written, by Professor W. H. New, University of British Columbia.

19 John Wain, "Another Room in Hell", *Atlantic* CCXXII (August 1968), 84–6.

20 Walter Allen, "The Masterpiece of the Forties", *On Contemporary Literature*, ed. Richard Kostelanetz (New York, 1964), pp. 419–21.

21 Anthony Burgess, "Europe's Day of the Dead", *Spectator* (20 January 1967), p. 74.

22 *Prairie Schooner: Malcolm Lowry Issue* XXXVII, 4 (Winter 1963–4).

23 From Douglas Day's inscription in my copy of his biography of Lowry.

24 Douglas Day, *Malcolm Lowry*, *op. cit.*, pp. 326–50. Subsequent references to Professor Day's biography will be indicated by page number in brackets.

25 Heilman, review, *op. cit.*, p. 492.

26 David Markson, "Malcolm Lowry: A Reminiscence", *The Nation* (7 February 1966), 164–7.

27 As this book went to press, David Markson's study appeared (April 1978): *Malcolm Lowry's Volcano: Myth, Symbol, Meaning* (New York).

2

Tragedy as a Meditation on Itself: Reflexiveness in *Under the Volcano*

by STEPHEN TIFFT

Under the Volcano moves toward catastrophe with classical direcness. Yet a baroque system of analogies continuously modifies and complicates the novel's tragic design; moreover, Firmin's awareness of his self-determined role further belies the apparent simplicity of the tragedy. If Lowry has managed to coordinate all the analogical substructures, however, we ought to find their unifying principle at the core of this novel's particular definition of tragedy. Many have pointed to the basic tragic shape of *Under the Volcano*, but few have attended to the reasons for the fall or the way it comes about; but only by doing so can we discern the novel's essential tragic principle.

According to two common but fallacious interpretations, the crux of the Consul's tragedy is either alcoholism, or the inability to love. These theories are easily dispensed with. The first maintains that Firmin's "tragic" purpose is merely to have another drink—that the idea of tragedy is itself a rationalization projected by the Consul. But Lowry takes pains to attribute only a relatively small proportion of the Consul's suffering, whether on the political, the domestic, or any other level of the tragedy, directly to alcoholism. The Consul's consciousness of his broad catastrophic pattern is sufficient to raise him above the pathos of mere alcoholism, and he even draws a certain qualified grandeur from his tragic heritage. The second and more interesting interpretation defines the Consul's *hamartia* by reference to the recurrent theme, *"no se puede vivir sin amar"* (one cannot live

46

without loving). The maxim certainly carries symbolic weight, but it serves little purpose as a formulation of Firmin's tragic flaw. Only by resorting to shifting definitions of "loving" can one convert the theme from one level of tragic analogy to another; and making excessive claims for the theme of *"no se puede . . ."* too often leads one to ascribe to Lowry a saccharine argument for Good Samaritanism, surely beyond what the text warrants. Lowry's ironic handling of the Good Samaritan theme, and especially of its manifestation in Hugh as a foil to the Consul, bespeaks an ambivalence that can hardly be ignored.

So much for the false *hamartia*. Tragedy turns on a purpose held or an action undertaken by the protagonist, whether such purpose or action be an error or not. The crux of tragedy is the intimate relation between this purpose or action and the catastrophe which issues from it inevitably. Although the inevitability results from special conditions in the given world of each tragedy, the tragic action originates solely with the protagonist. Firmin's manifold tragedy comprises two independent downfalls, the rupture of his reconciliation with Yvonne and his murder by the fascists. Furthermore, he endures throughout a postlapsarian state of continuous suffering, like that of Prometheus. A single tragic purpose propels the Consul's multiple tragedy.

That purpose, the essence of the tragic definition of *Under the Volcano*, is as follows: the Consul dedicates himself to the tragic destiny which—he is convinced—is his.

It will be immediately evident that this tragic purpose is purely reflexive—tragedy proceeds from the conviction that it must proceed. This is an elegant refinement of the tragic mode: tragedy as a meditation on itself. The Consul's purpose may sound tautological, but it is not. Firmin's fidelity to his doom does not amount to the same thing as the catastrophe itself; only within the given world of the novel is his tragic purpose lethal. Seen as a *hamartia* within that world, the Consul's reflexive preoccupation with tragedy is characterized by a curiously inverted form of hubris: his powerful, obsessed mind does not soar, but plummets; it sets him apart from normal society nonetheless.

If the tragic purpose I have suggested is correct, it will give access to the working out of the Consul's tragedy within each of the major analogical substructures. Arguing for a *"Gestalt* reading"[1] of *Under the Volcano*, Douglas Day suggests five levels on which such a reading might proceed: chthonic, human, political, magical, and religious. Adapting the scheme to levels of tragedy, we can organize the analogical substructures into the following categories: interpersonal, religious, occult, mythical/literary, and political. In this way we can account for not only the two major *mythoi* (in Frye's sense of narrative patterns)—namely the Yvonne-Geoffrey catastrophe and the political plot that culminates at El Farolito—but also three main sorts of tragic motif. Though these levels of the Consul's tragedy present slightly different landscapes, they have in common his one paradigmatic tragic purpose: to remain faithful to his tragic destiny.

We are left with an important question: What does Lowry mean by creating a character who reads his own tragedy concurrently with the reader? Lowry conceived of the Consul's tragic reflexiveness as far more than cement for the artifice. The idea of reflexiveness and the way reflexive perception can affect reality permeate Lowry's presentation of character, his theory of art, his mimesis of reality—even perhaps his own experience of reality. The Consul's reflexiveness not only unifies the structural elements of the novel, but is also its main subject. *Under the Volcano* is not merely an artifice that counterfeits reality: by describing tragedy as a meditation on tragedy, by blurring the boundaries between fictive interpretation and concrete experience, the novel continually inverts fiction and reality.

Although Lowry never fully reveals the origins of the Consul's tragic fatalism, they are suggested in the way Firmin's reflexiveness affects the crucial events of the domestic tragedy. His tragic conviction that all is lost frustrates each attempt at reconciliation with Yvonne and creates a vicious circle in which his actions can only lead to impasses which reinforce prior assumptions. The Consul recognizes something like this cycle of frustration at the heart of his drinking problem:

> ". . . the whole trouble being as we see it that Yvonne's long-dreamed-of coming alas but put away the anguish my boy there's nothing in it," the voice gabbled on, "has in itself created the most important situation in your life save one namely the far more important situation it in turn creates of your having to have five hundred drinks in order to deal with it. . . ."[2]

48

Indeed, this vicious circle—perhaps a spiral would be a more apt figure—serves as a paradigm of the tragic action in general. Propelled by his fatalism, the Consul cycles through repeated rounds of guilt-resentment-withdrawal-guilt as he approaches catastrophe.

The reasons for Firmin's guilt over his treatment of Yvonne are obvious. What is less evident, but crucial, is the way a free-floating sense of guilt—a pure guilt, prior to any culpability—cripples his actions before he can take them. In its clearest manifestations, this abstract guilt is secreted whenever an impending performance overwhelms the Consul with a premature sense of failure. During his abortive attempt to make love with his wife, for example, Firmin's guilty longing for escape, which cannot be attributed solely to alcoholic craving, precedes his impotence with Yvonne. Evidently his dread of failure has ensured it (he later succeeds with María when considerably more drunk; the stakes are lower then). Lowry alludes to Firmin's dread of performance, which leads to guilt in advance of its earning, at most of the pivotal moments in the domestic plot. The motif most frequently employed is the "Hell Bunker", where, in Firmin's youth, another abortive sexual performance was discovered (this event is neatly tied by its location to Geoffrey's obsessed, successful performance as a boy golfer).

Like his sexual endeavours, the Consul's drinking, or rather his attempt to carry it off, is one life-long performance, a point Lowry likes to convey by referring to the Consul's erect bearing in almost all conditions. Thus Geoffrey's humiliation in the Hell Bunker is compounded when subsequently, with all eyes upon him, he is refused drinks at a pub significantly named "The Case Is Altered". He spends the rest of his life making good the failure. Turning to the crucial rejection of Yvonne's white flag in Chapter VII, we find Lowry employing this double motif of performance anxiety to its greatest possible effect at the moment when the Consul knows reconciliation to be incumbent upon him. Whether Lowry means to attribute the Consul's performance anxiety to sexual guilt, or to guilt at failing to live up to the standards set by his surrogate family, the Taskersons, he expresses it in fatalistic terms, as a kind of speculation in guilt which yields devastating dividends.

The Consul requires a lover who will demonstrate absolute acceptance of him whatever he does, one "who, upon that last and final green, though I hole out in four, accepts my ten and three score. . . . Though I have more" (p. 203). Despite Yvonne's commitment to Geoffrey, she has blundered badly by betraying him with Hugh and then with Laruelle. She certainly had good reason to do so, but she seems unaware of the ways in which her infidelity has reinforced some of the Consul's overwhelming insecurities, and so has increased his fatalism. Her efforts to retrieve the marriage always waver at the crucial moments, through her own fatalism, and she too effectively blocks reconciliation with her faulty and untested assumptions—a point that is frequently overlooked. The following passage, for example, is often cited as the best expression of the attractions that induce the Consul to choose alcohol over his wife.

> . . . for not even the gates of heaven, opening wide to receive me, could fill me with such celestial complicated and hopeless joy as the iron screen that rolls up with a crash, as the unpadlocked jostling jalousies which admit those whose souls tremble with the drinks they carry unsteadily to their lips.
>
> (p. 50)

In fact, these are Yvonne's thoughts. Within minutes of her arrival in Quauhnahuac, she has already assumed that Geoffrey is rejecting her appeal, and imagines this as his explanation for the denial. For all her hope, Yvonne starts the day with fatalistic assumptions that will fulfill themselves by nightfall.

Lowry is careful to link Firmin's feeling of betrayal, and with it his fatalistic sense of his own perdition as a tragic figure, to psychological configurations established deep in his past. As a child Geoffrey had suffered from the death of his mother and abandonment by his father; from these traumata his tragic worldview began to evolve. The Consul frequently follows up thoughts of Yvonne's betrayal of him with allusions to this early abandonment. He cannot forgive those who were supposed to take care of him and did not: his father, or in a loftier sense, God; and his stepmother, or Yvonne. At the pivotal moment in Chapter VII, when he is alone with Yvonne at Jacques' house, and on the brink of reconciliation, the Consul reveals again the subconscious link between betrayal and childhood abandonment:

> "I do love you. Only—" "I can never forgive you deeply enough": was that what was in his mind to add?

—And yet, he was thinking all over again, and all over as for the first time, how he had suffered, suffered, suffered without her; indeed such desolation, such a desperate sense of abandonment, bereavement, as during this last year without Yvonne, he had never known in his life, unless it was when his mother died.

(pp. 197–8)

From his childhood the Consul has had a fatalistic distrust of the possibility of anyone's understanding devotion to him, which allows him to see perfect logic in Yvonne's infidelity. Nonetheless, he has consistently craved such devotion, and his reaction when he does not receive it is profound, unforgiving resentment. When "abandoned", that is, not accepted without question, he takes umbrage at the wrong-doing of the beloved; his guilt leads to his resentment, Yvonne's infidelity being a useful bridge. The process is intensified by her campaign to save him, which he resents because it forces him to admit his culpability—thus aggravating his guilt—and because of the implication that Yvonne is less at fault than he would like her to be. Resentment immediately precedes each of the major breakdowns of the reconciliation.

Withdrawal follows resentment. The Consul thinks of withdrawal as a form of self-reliance, a thumbing of the nose at the loved ones on whom he had so dangerously depended. Actually it is an expedient closer to escape. His chief avenue of escape is drinking, which escalates with each successive crisis. Yet the Consul manages to turn his hallucinatory voyages into Dionysian celebrations of dissolution which supercede the pathos of mere escape. As he sublimates the impulse to withdraw, in the form of a grand Dionysian gesture, the Consul attains to the impersonality that he needs as a tragic protagonist: he withdraws not simply from Yvonne, but from the world. But the Dionysian cannot avoid extremity. The apotheosis of impersonality is the absolute dissolution of self; withdrawal from the world must finally be physical as well as mental. Although the Consul moves toward the abyss in logical fulfillment of a mythic withdrawal, he has started merely by withdrawing from Yvonne, and the larger tragedy may be more than he bargains for. As a compromise he reiterates the eremitic motif of William Blackstone, renouncer of civilization, but Sr. Chief of Rostrums Zuzugoitea rejects the compromise and ushers the Consul to the ultimate withdrawal.

Although the Consul wavers between an innocuous eremitism

51

and a visionary self-destructiveness, in either case his last with-drawal from Yvonne is decisive. He breaks with her when he flees the Salón Ofélia and completes the interpersonal catastrophe at El Farolito by sullying himself with the whore María. A fatalistic resentment seems to master him, yet he rejects the waning possibility of reconciliation deliberately:

> . . . some reckless murderous power was drawing him on, forcing him, while he yet remained passionately aware of the all too possible consequences and somehow as innocently unconscious, to do without precaution or conscience what he would never be able to undo or gainsay . . .
> So this was it, the final stupid unprophylactic rejection. He could prevent it even now. He would not prevent it.
>
> (p. 348)

Just beneath the surface of the Consul's conviction of the finality of his act, a hint of guilt appears in the suggestion of venereal disease. The reader may feel that objectively Firmin is wrong about Yvonne's unforgiveness, but the Consul's guilt tends always to lead him to ensure the accuracy of his misgivings, transforming the subjective into the objective. If his fornication with María makes him feel so guilty that the thought of reconciliation is intolerable, then the act *is* final: "But now too at least this much was clear. He couldn't go back to Yvonne if he wanted to" (p. 353).

This sort of self-fulfilling prophecy could generally be corrected if the Consul and Yvonne were simply to confide in one another. But as Lowry presents it human interaction is constantly beset by crossed signals and blockages of communication, whose pervasiveness he stresses by making them a part of his narrative technique. Each chapter imprisons us within a particular mind, underscoring each character's difficulty in trying to understand the others. To escape one's subjectivity and make contact with another requires an enormous leap of faith, but a conviction of doom blocks such a leap. This crippling fatalism hampers even Yvonne's optimism, and is insuperable in the Consul's case. The hopeless round of guilt, resentment, and withdrawal is woven into the fabric of the Consul's being, as he knows. He does not recognize so clearly that his inbred fatalism infects the future as well. Even when all was going well, he could not shake off a sense of doom which compelled him to see catastrophe in the fact of happiness:

> Far too soon their life together had begun to seem too much of a triumph, it had been too good, too horribly unimaginable to lose, impossible finally to bear: it was as if it had become itself its own foreboding that it could not last, a foreboding that was like a presence too, turning his steps towards the taverns again.
>
> (p. 201)

The mixture of fatalism and guilty resentment that poisons the Consul's last chance for a reconciliation with Yvonne also compels him to reject help from other quarters, especially from figures of authority. Lowry deepens the significance of this spiritual ailment by extending the principle to the level of religious analogy, in the motif of the Consul's fall from God's grace. The epigraph that Lowry selects from the work of John Bunyan underscores the religious analogy as a paradigm for all aspects of Firmin's tragedy:

> . . . animals had no soul to perish under the everlasting weight of Hell or Sin, as mine was like to do . . . yet that which was added to my sorrow was, that I could not find with all my soul that I did desire deliverance.

Bunyan was heavily influenced by Calvin, and the Calvinist doctrine of predestination provides another apt context for the fatalism and the unanchored sense of guilt discussed in the last section. Like Bunyan in the first half of his autobiography, *Grace Abounding to the Chief of Sinners*, the Consul feels that he is a predestined reprobate, and the conviction throttles repentance; his constant preoccupation with the possible signs of his sinful state mires him deeper in hopelessness.

Sin is the stigma of a reprobate, but Lowry handles the concept of sin obliquely. Numerous allusions identify the Consul as an avatar of Adam; having no such clearly defined sin as that of Adam, the Consul assumes for Adam a surrogate sin—the ingratitude of hating the Garden:

> And of course the real *reason* for that punishment . . . might well have been that the poor fellow, who knows, secretly loathed

53

the place! Simply hated it, and had done so all along. *And that the Old Man found this out....*

(p. 134)

The Consul, in the guise of Adam, expresses his sense of sin by rejecting the salvation God offers, just as he had rejected Yvonne and her help. Again the Consul's consciousness of his own ingratitude makes him feel guilty. Guilt in general is the Consul's Pavlovian response to any thought of God. Firmin mentions repeatedly the sunflower which "Stares. Fiercely. All day. Like God!" (p. 179). God's stare is not innocuous: "I know [the sunflower] watches me and I know it hates me" (p. 144). The garden is the prime locale for the Consul's guilty certainty of God's surveillance. But like his guilt toward Yvonne, the Consul's guilt before God is general—disproportionate to and often quite detached from any of his actions. In this respect guilt is like original sin, a fact of the Consul's being independent of his actual behaviour. Where there is no cause for guilt, he will invent one—like the *Samaritan* incident.

Bunyan's guilt made him so ashamed that he could not bear to pray to God. Shame may also help to explain the Consul's inhibition: "Christ . . . would help you if you asked him: you cannot ask him" (p. 65). But there is a further explanation: fatalism convinces both men that prayer is useless. Bunyan despairs, "now to pray, seeing God has cast you off, is the next way to anger and offend him more than you ever did before;"[3] the Consul echoes, "God has little patience with remorse!" (p. 79). The Consul would prefer to flee all contact—hence his vicarious loathing of Paradise. Thus the faltalism of guilt can be seen as the cause, as well as the result, of Firmin/Adam's ingratitude.

The Consul's unorthodox meditations on Adam's expulsion are touched off by his drunken misreading of the sign, *"¿Le gusta este jardin que es suyo? ¡Evite que sus hijos lo destruyan!,"* as "You like this garden? Why is it yours? We evict those who destroy!" (p. 128).[4] Drawing on Thomas Burnet's description of the earth as a Paradise damaged by sin,[5] Lowry links the motif of the ruined garden to the Consul's ungrateful loathing for his Paradise, and presents the ruined garden as a subjective and individual phenomenon: Mr. Quincey's garden, unlike the Consul's, is neatly kept. In his exposition of the Paradise myth to Mr. Quincey, the Consul interprets eviction as loosely as destruction. The eviction is not physical but spiritual: "his punishment really consisted . . . in his having to *go on living there*, alone, of course—suffering, unseen, cut off from God" (p. 133). Thus the sin and the punishment are virtually the same—hating the Garden that God provided. By construing this hatred as punishment, the Consul manages to find in it fresh evidence of his guilt, thereby perpetuating and intensifying the whole cycle.

Lowry has arranged his religious motifs as a closed circuit which illustrates perfectly the Consul's compulsion to fuel his own reflexive tragedy: the Consul ruins his garden by the "sin" of hating it; he hates it because his guilt makes him perceive it as ruined. By this subjective, fatalistic vicious circle we return to the Calvinist doctrine of predestination. The Consul believes that he is one of the reprobate, rather than one of the elect. He will therefore do nothing to save himself, but will occupy himself only in looking for indications of his reprobation. His pride will not permit him to endure the shame of a confrontation with God, so convinced is he of the outcome of such a confrontation; he prefers, like the lost souls of Canto II of Dante's *Inferno*, to rush eagerly toward Hell. His sin, like that of Marlowe's Faustus, is the sin against the Holy Ghost—"pride and despair, inextricably linked".[6]

Lowry relates the level of occult analogy to the religious through the imagery of the Cabbala, the focus of the Consul's interest in the occult: "the Cabbala is sometimes considered as the garden itself, with the Tree of Life . . . planted within it."[7] Yet it is difficult to take the occult as seriously as the religious parallel, partly because Lowry seems to use black magic without full conviction as an apologetic tactic to ennoble the Consul's drunkenness—and a melodramatic tactic at that. By the time we are introduced to the Consul, his metaphorical fall from mystical power has already occurred. He has abandoned his book on "Secret Knowledge", and magic, black or white, has abandoned him. Nevertheless, we can reconstruct some of the factors in his occult fall, and so observe the Consul's tragedy from several new slants.

We can arrive at the most important of these new perspectives via one idea which Lowry propounds throughout his occult analogies—that the Consul's infernal experience is valuable and even desirable. Lowry hints at this in maintaining that "the agonies of the drunkard find their most accurate poetic analogue in the agonies of the mystic who has abused his powers."[8] Lowry draws here on William James' *The Varieties of Religious Experience*, wherein James stresses the alcoholic's capacity for mystical insight; alcohol provides momentary access to truth. The connection between alcohol and spiritual truth lies deep in the Cabbalist tradition:

> The Cabbalists regard wine as the outstanding symbol of creation, the guarded words that have never been revealed to man, the hidden spiritual energy underlying all things.[9]

The Consul, following the example of Rimbaud, flirts with particularly hellish forms of mystical insight. Perle Epstein points out[10] that Rimbaud and other *poètes maudits* are close to Cabbalism in valuing the experience of hell, or at least of evil. Since the mystic can learn by exposure to evil that it is another of God's many manifestations, infernal experience can be another way to heaven.

Rimbaud's world is based in the inverted cosmological hierarchy of Romanticism, where the divine is sought in internal depths and the sky-god is a malevolent, repressive figure.[11] But Lowry uses inversion as an index of sickness; he can be distinguished from Rimbaud in this: that his attitude toward inversion is not prescriptive. He believes in an essentially Christian hierarchy. Thus he is happy to follow the stern Cabbalistic conception of inversion— the inversion of the Sephirotic Tree. The Tree is a hierarchy of divine emanations, which the Cabbalist strives to climb to reach *Kether*, the Crown, and salvation. But when the adept violates the Cabbalistic code, he is punished: the Tree becomes inverted, so that his efforts to climb bring him not toward *Kether*, but toward *Oliphoth*, the abyss of husks and demons. Then his striving itself hastens catastrophe.

The inversion of the Sephirotic Tree overthrows the Consul. The hope of attaining holiness through the experience of evil is illusory for him, since he has abused his occult powers. Because of the spiritual significance of wine in the Cabbala, its abuse by the Consul is a terrible sacrilege.[12] His drinking exemplifies the inversion of salvation and punishment: once a means of attaining spiritual enlightenment, drinking now blackens his soul at an increasing pace. The Consul seems to have stalled halfway through his mystical quest, incapacitated by his tragic reflexiveness. Setting out to attain holiness through the vision of hell, he began to believe in that vision as the reality in which he was destined to remain, instead of knowing it to be an illusion which he would transcend. His mistake was that of Rimbaud: *"Je me crois en enfer, donc j'y suis."*[13] This constitutes the Cabbalistic sin of imbalance, "mistaking appearance for reality"[14] ("my equilibrium, and equilibrium is all, precarious," he misgives belatedly). In this way, the Consul has been transformed from a white into a black magician, one whose depravity makes him see the infernal as a source of power as well as an end in itself.

By the opening of the novel, however, the Consul can no longer consider himself even a black magician. Bereft of his power, he is often inclined to imagine himself a pure victim, chosen without intelligible reason by the pitiless gods, a prisoner of *La Máquina Infernal.* But although the Consul would enjoy the luxury of regarding himself as an innocent victim, ultimately he cannot do so. He knows that the infernal machine is a deserved nemesis, and that his rightful spiritual domain is the *Qliphoth.* Despite moments of penitence, he has developed a fatalistic relish for his climb up the inverted Tree toward the abyss, and he gives himself up to the infernal machine that encages him:

> Let it go! There was a kind of fierce delight in this final acceptance. Let everything go!
>
> (pp. 222–23)

Close examination suggests that Lowry used most of his analogies to myths and literature with a purposeful complexity that might not be suspected on a superficial reading. With surprising consistency the most important *mythoi* develop the theme of the Consul's tragic reflexiveness and explore its implications.

The Faust parallel is one of the most complicated, yet rewarding, of the mythic analogies. Lowry refers explicitly to the two major versions of the Faust myth, Marlowe's and Goethe's. He perceived that the former is a tragedy, and the latter a divine comedy culminating in Faust's salvation, and he employed them differently. The Consul is much closer to Marlowe's Faustus than to Goethe's Faust. Faustus made his pact with the devil in order to attain a kind of knowledge and power amounting basically to black magic, with a bit of geography thrown in. In the case of the Consul, the Faustus parallel also touches on black magic. But its chief interest lies in its illumination of the reasons not for the pact, but for Faustus' failure to repent. Marlowe vacillates in presenting the motivations for this failure, but finally he settles on despair. Despite the Good Angel's exhortations to the contrary (parralleling those of Firmin's Good Angel) Faustus, like the Consul, believes the hour too late for repentance, and his offence too great. Their common impulse is rather to hide than to repent (like the Consul's Adam): "Then will I headlong fly into the earth," as Laruelle misreads Marlowe. So convinced is the Consul of the certainty of damnation, that his attitude resembles that of Mephistopheles as much as that of Faustus: "Why this is hell, nor am I out of it."

The theme of Goethe's *Faust* is almost the diametric opposite of that of *Doctor Faustus*: "Whosoever unceasingly strives upward . . . him can we save." Lowry emphasizes the significance of this theme to the Consul's tragedy by using it as an epigraph to the novel; but he clearly dissociates the Consul from salvation when he juxtaposes the epigraph from Bunyan (quoted above) illustrating despair. To strive unceasingly is precisely what the Consul fails to do. Faust is led to his pact through despair, not of attaining salvation, but of learning *"was die Welt/ Im Innersten zusammen hält."*[15] Goethe ingeniously creates a pact in which the devil may have Faust's soul only if Faust becomes satisfied with his state of knowledge and stops striving. His despair is thus a spur to further striving. Lowry astutely bases the Consul's tragedy on qualities precisely the opposite of Faust's: the Consul falls because, unlike Faust, he is resigned, even committed to his despair.[16]

Lowry goes to great lengths to elaborate the complementarity of the Consul and Hugh. Their differences make the half-brothers nearly mirror images of one another. Thus Hugh with his idealism echoes the aspiration, now lost, of Geoffrey's youth. The Faust (as opposed to the Faustus) parallel applies to Hugh rather than to the Consul. Hugh's efforts to save the world always come to naught; but his striving continues unabated—presumably even after the calamity at Parián. His Faustian (and political) model is Juan Cerillo: "For man, every man, Juan seemed to be telling him, even as Mexico, must ceaselessly struggle upward" (p. 108).

Despite the kind of occasional lapses we have suggested above, Yvonne shares this saving grace, and Lowry consciously (and melodramatically) imitates Goethe[17] in arranging for Yvonne in Chapter XI a divine assumption patterned on that of Faust's innocent lover, Gretchen; in both cases, salvation is a reward for fidelity to a lost soul. In marked contrast to Hugh and Yvonne, the Consul knows that he has lost the faith and the hope of salvation that he once had "When he had striven upwards, as at the beginning with Yvonne" (p. 361).

The parallel with Dante's *Inferno* reiterates this contrast between the Consul and Hugh.[18] The Consul is already a lost soul; Lowry presents Hugh as an avatar of Dante, though with little conviction. It is Hugh who places himself in the role of Dante— "*Nel mezzo del* bloody *cammin di nostra vita mi ritrovai* in . . ." (p. 150)—and he, not the Consul, is seeking the proper path. Hugh is headed toward Vera Cruz (the True Cross) at the end of the novel, though we are allowed to remain skeptical about his spiritual arrival. On the other hand, very few of the allusions to the *Inferno* occur in connexion with the Consul, and those that do serve as no more than a shorthand for damnation. The bells tolling "*Dolente . . . Dolore*" at the Consul's death are quoting the inscription over the Gates of Hell in Dante, which ends, "Abandon every hope, ye that enter".

The Consul is lost because he finds the *Inferno* an end in itself. Dante's quest falls into the class of myths that Frye calls the "Eros myth", that of the climb toward spiritual enlightenment. The Consul's fault in this regard not only defines his difference from Dante (and Hugh); it also gives us the broader meaning of *no se puede vivir sin amar*. Here *amar* carries all the climbing, questing, striving, living significance of Eros—it is the life principle, opposed to the Consul's resignation, sterility, and hopelessness. The Consul clearly gives *amar* this sense in his desperate prayer: "Teach me to love again, to love life" (p. 289).

Recognizing the inevitability of his suffering, the Consul attempts to excuse his complacency, from time to time, by thinking of himself as a latter-day Prometheus. The parallel is played out largely in the confrontation with Laruelle at the Paris Café. Grandiloquently, the Consul defends his drinking as "My battle for the survival of the human consciousness" (p. 217); only in this way can he appear to be a Promethean hero. More realistically, the Promethean parallel operates best not in the context of service to mankind, but in that of voluntary isolation from one's peers. Prometheus refused humility before Zeus, willingly underwent solitary punishment, and was thrown into the abyss for his pains; and it is in his similar defiance that the Consul most resembles Prometheus. The Consul derives a certain comfort from the feeling that his suffering, like that of Prometheus, is inevitable. Laruelle remarks pointedly, *"Je crois que la vautour est doux à Prometheus et que les Ixion se plaisent en Enfers."*[19] The Consul is happiest, perhaps, when he feels locked into his torment (for reasons less noble than those of Prometheus), and this is another affinity with the god.

Potentially, a Christ parallel would also enable the Consul to rationalize his suffering as self-willed, borne for the sake of mankind. The Consul himself, however, is unable to swallow the analogy. Jocularly he declaims to a pariah dog, "Yet this day, pichicho, shalt thou be with me in—" (p. 229), and watches as the dog hops away, terrified at the anti-Christian implications. Analogies to Christ generally call up in the Consul an amused self-irony; he feels closer to the Antichrist, who recurs in numerical form as 666, the Beast of Revelation. The association ultimately redounds on him, when Zuzugoitea calls him the *antichrista.*

The Christ parallel is actually introduced by Hugh (p. 111), and is employed rather to establish Hugh as a Judas than the Consul as a Christ. Thus most of the allusions to Christ involve His betrayal. The Consul sinks comfortably into the effortless inevitability of the betrayed man. He defines Christ by His betrayal— "and betrayed Christ into being" (pp. 286–7). The Consul's betrayal, seen as part of a divine plan, makes things much easier for him.

Lowry draws analogies from three Shakespearean tragedies, each shedding light on a different aspect of the Consul's tragic vision. During a hiatus in his conversation with Mr. Quincey, the Consul, himself withdrawn into an alcoholic swoon, aptly recalls Thomas De Quincey's reading of a Macbeth "insulated, self-withdrawn into a deep syncope and suspension of earthly passion" (p. 136); De Quincey's words reflect the Consul's own distance from reality, within his tragic limbo. Macbeth is moved to murder by the witches' prophesies of his future titles; he sees projected before him his destiny—without the calamity that attends it—and bases his tragic actions on the credence he gives that projection. The Consul also projects a destiny, based not on intimations of nobility but on "portents of doom, of the heart failing" (p. 284). Like Macbeth, the Consul brings his world down on his head by trying consciously to fulfil what appears to him an ineluctable fate. And like Macbeth, he soon loses the ability of determine whether the origin of his vision is within or without.

The analogy to *Othello* is simpler and more direct. Firmin plays the parts of Othello and of Iago simultaneously. Convinced that Hugh and Yvonne are in the process of betraying him afresh, the Consul spurs his rage by incorporating Iago's words to Othello into his own denunciation of Yvonne:

> But even if Hugh makes the most of it again it won't be long, it won't be long, before he realizes he's only one of the hundred or so other ninneyhammers with gills like codfish and veins like racehorses—prime as goats all of them, hot as monkeys, salt as wolves in pride!
>
> (p. 313)

He then doubles the potency of his jealousy by association his supposed sexual betrayal with the "plot" to save him:

> What an uncommon time you two must have had, paddling palms and playing bubbies and titties all day under cover of saving me. . . .
>
> (p. 313)

The allusion to *Othello* provide an effective example of the way the Consul's tragic tendency of mind reaps its own reward.

The Consul's fraternal and conjugal relationships rupture finally at the Sálon Ofélia. Ophelia and Gertrude, with the rich complexities of their relations with Hamlet, are telescoped in Yvonne, while the Consul bears a marked resemblance to Hamlet, both *père* and *fils*. In some respects an innocent victim of a man single-mindedly withdrawn into "an antic disposition", Yvonne also shares with Ophelia the humiliation of her lover's cruel slurs. Her rejection by the Consul carries some of the perplexity and anguish of Ophelia's; yet she is not so spotless a victim as Ophelia. By directing our perspective toward Yvonne's culpability, we see the Hamlet *père*/Gertrude/Claudius triangle emerging in place of the Hamlet/Ophelia constellation. This aspect of the tragedy stresses the Consul's innocence rather than Yvonne's. Though the sense of a plot against the husband remains, Lowry shifts the guilt from brother to wife, since it would suit his purpose ill to taint Hugh with the purposeful villainy of a Claudius. The emphasis is not on usurpation but on adultery. The Consul is father and son at once: he is betrayed, but instead of being murdered like the King, he grows sick at soul like the Prince. And it is Prince Hamlet's profound disgust that permeates the Consul's feelings about Yvonne, Hugh, and Jacques:

> But the abominable impact on his whole being at this moment of the fact that that hideously elongated cucumiform bundle of blue nerves and gills below [Laruelle's] steaming unselconscious stomach had sought its pleasure in his wife's body brought him trembling to his feet. How loathsome, how incredibly loathsome was reality.
>
> (p. 207)

The loathsomeness of reality paralyses Hamlet, and it is one of the causes of the Consul's paralysis too. Like the Consul, Hamlet longs to withdraw: "O God, I could be bounded in a nut-shell and count myself a king of infinite space, were it not that I have bad dreams." While Hamlet contemplates suicide, the Consul opts for alcohol, which he paradoxically aligns with being rather than with withdrawal: "To drink or not to drink" (p. 287). The rotten world which paralyses the Consul encompasses far more than bestial passions and human betrayal—the very fabric of society is rotten:

> Fie on't! Ah, fie! 'tis an unweeded garden
> That grows to seed: things rank and gross in nature
> Possess it merely.

Both Hamlet and the Consul see the world as a ruined garden. For them the disease of their respective times infects the family, the state, and even the soul of mankind; and they see it in its largest aspect—as a fall from paradise.

Acceptance of the tragic lot ushers in catastrophe on the level of political analogy as surely as on any other. The causal connexion between tragic reflexiveness and the political tragedy presents itself most clearly in the way the Consul's murder comes about. Lowry provides unmistakable evidence at numerous points that the Consul knows well what iron fist rules Parián—the fascist *Union Militar*, led locally by Sanabria and Zuzugoitea. Despite this, and despite the fact that "the Consul was more afraid of the police than death" (p. 225), he goes deliberately "into that glorious Parián wilderness . . . towards ineluctable personal disaster" (p. 139)—a disaster he actively seeks after the fiasco at the Salón Ofélia. Zuzugoitea's finding Hugh's anarchist card on the Consul may seem merely fortuitous, though crucial; but the card is the last piece of a great deal of evidence gathered by the fascists. The Consul is a marked man, a consul in a country where consuls are thought to be spies, and one who has remained after his country has broken diplomatic relations with Mexico. (The Consul's decision to stay in Mexico, which he himself recognizes as a surrender to tragic fate, is the first step in the political tragedy.) The fascists have kept up on him to the extent of knowing that he is a cuckold (p. 369), and seem to have been waiting for a convenient excuse to lock him up. In defiance of his parlous state, the Consul remains in the bar, entranced by his doom, providing such excuses until his assumption that "it's too late" proves correct. Then he exchanges imprisonment for death by attacking the police and freeing the horse.

These are the mechanics of the Consul's catastrophe on the political level. But Lowry also uses that personal tragedy as a metaphor for a tragedy engulfing not only Mexico but the world at large.

We have seen the operation of the eremitic instinct on the interpersonal and the religious levels of the Consul's tragedy: when faced with his sins and shortcomings, and with the responsibility for their correction, the Consul tends to withdraw from the challenge, feeling unequal to it. This applies equally to political responsibility. He sees little hope for the world, and his solution is to try to be left alone. His incognito is William Blackstone, a colonial settler who escaped society to seek asylum among the Indians, and then withdrew from them to total solitude. The Consul characterizes all of the influences from which he is escaping under the title, "fellows with ideas", i.e. those who would try to correct him, help him, or otherwise remind him of his responsibilities; or more generally, those who, unlike him, do not believe that their cause is lost. The modern wilderness to which he escapes is hidden within himself: " '*Now*, little cat,' the Consul tapped his chest indicatively . . . 'the Indians are in here' " (p. 135). The Consul's problem is that an internal wilderness does not provide enough shelter. He takes the fascists for Indians, but "The only trouble was one was very much afraid these particular Indians might turn out to be people with ideas too" (p. 358).

Hugh, in contrast to the Consul, helps to demonstrate the absurdity and peril of his brother's fatalistic isolationism. We have seen that Hugh evinces a Goethean striving for political amelioration; the dramatization of this worthy quality is his attempt to help the Indian dying on the wayside. We must be careful with Hugh's idealism, however, for Lowry qualifies and even mocks it on several fronts. Of Hugh's brush with the vigilantes, the Consul remarks drily, "Never mind, old boy, it would have been worse than the windmills" (p. 248). Beyond his Quixotic impracticality, Hugh can be criticized for his failure to live up to his principles, as he himself knows too well. His guilt over his failure to *act* recurs through the motif, "They are losing the Battle of the Ebro." He associates revolutionary songs with men of principled action like Juan Cerillo, but while he is drunkenly singing these songs in the woods, both Yvonne and the Consul are dying.

Nonetheless, the mere desire to achieve good is preferable to the Consul's fatalistic, *laissez-faire* determinism:

> Why should anybody interfere with anybody? . . .
> . . . Can't you see there's a sort of determinism about the fate of nations? They all seem to get what they deserve in the long run.
> . . . Read history. Go back a thousand years. What is the use of interfering with its worthless stupid course? (pp. 309–10)

Such fatalism will have tragic consequences—for Mexico as well as for the Consul. In the wayside incident Mexican law hamstrings the Mexican people—no one is allowed to help the Indian because such aid would make one an accessory after the fact. And ironically, the police and even the taxicab drivers are of no help to those they should serve, because they are all on strike. Here the Consul's theory of non-intervention, modified slightly as the peasant women's ethic of prudence, runs aground:

> And yet, in these old women it was as if, through the various tragedies of Mexican history, pity, the impulse to approach, and terror, the impulse to escape (as one had learned at college),

having replaced it, had finally been reconciled by prudence, the
conviction it is better to stay where you are . . .

And the truth was, it was perhaps one of those occasions when
nothing *would* have done any good. Which only made it worse
than ever.

(pp. 248–9)

Lowry explicitly formulates the historical issue according to his
tragic paradigm. Similarly, he applies to Mexico the related theme
of the Consul's self-victimization. The Indian is a payroll rider for
the National Bank of Ejido Credit, which was part of President
Cárdenas' policy of agrarian reform in the late thirties, providing
funds for collective farming. This was a prime target for fascist
groups, who hindered the programme by hiring vigilantes of the
kind who, we assume, murdered the Indian. The self-victimization
of the Mexican people, then, is carried out by these vigilantes
and also in the person of the *pelado*, the low individual who steals
the money of the dying Indian, thus fulfilling the image of Mexico
preying upon herself—an image duplicated in references to the
traitorous Tlaxcalans. The prudence of the peasant women will
not help prevent this kind of abuse. Nor can the Consul's principles of withdrawal and of resignation to fate; he realizes this
suddenly as he dies, a victim of the fascists like the Ejido rider.[20] He
sees himself simultaneously as the bloody-handed *pelado*, a pre-
dator upon himself.

As Lowry has applied the Consul's destructive fatalism to
Mexico, he extends the theme to global relevance through the
Mexican fascists, whose connexion with Nazi Germany is made
clear at numerous points. As the fascists are a more menacing
version of the *pelado*, the analogue to the prudent old women and
the non-interfering Consul is Neville Chamberlain; hence the two
diplomatic cars which cruise serenely past the trouble at the wayside (pp. 246–7), shortly after Hugh has thought of the Munich
agreement (p. 239). The Consul serves as a link between the personal and the global: Hugh refers to his snore as "the muted
voice of England long asleep" (p. 98).

If the Consul's snoring is English, his drunkenness is universal,
a metaphor for the world's crazed self-destructiveness on the eve
of World War II. Hugh suggests that the world, like the Consul,
is chiefly concerned with evading its sense of guilt: "Good God,
if our civilization were to sober up for a couple of days, it'd die

of remorse on the third" (p. 117). The persistent symbol of world-guilt is the film *Las Manos de Orlac*, recurring throughout the novel by means of a poster showing the murderer's bloody hands, which Laruelle sees as "the hieroglyphic of the times. For really it was Germany itself" (p. 25). Hitler presides over the world's drunken nightmare like a Faust (p. 34) or a black magician (p. 186) —and in some ways, like the Consul.

Hugh finds Hitler less dangerous than the paralysis which seizes the world at his approach:

> . . . this world . . . was now pretending to be horrified at the very thing by which it proposed to be engulfed the first moment it could be perfectly certain the engulfing process would last long enough.
>
> (p. 154)

This passive complicity is identical to that of the Consul before his fate, and to that of the prudent bystanders at the wayside. Lowry suggests an interpretation of passive complicity which helps to explain both the helplessness of Hugh's idealism and the Consul's fatalism, and which touches again on the theme of a reflexive sense of tragedy:

> [the Indian] is, obviously, mankind himself, mankind dying— then, in the Battle of the Ebro, or now, in Europe, while we do nothing, or if we would, have put ourselves in a position where we *can* do nothing, but talk, while he goes on dying. . . .[21]

We have put *ourselves* in this position—for Lowry, this is the equivalent of the destruction of the Garden of Eden, and warrants ejection. The warning recurs at the end of the novel on the sign, "Do you like this garden, which is yours? See to it that your children do not destroy it!" But on the brink of war, mankind has already delivered the Garden over to the hands of Orlac: the *"Jefe de Jardineros"* ("Chief of Gardeners") is Fructuoso Sanabria, a Spanish fascist invited by traitorous elements in Mexico to exert his dark control over a fallen paradise. Sanabria reminds the Consul of his own former tenure of the unfallen garden at Granada; but now, sickened like Hamlet at the prospect of the unweeded garden, the Consul has lost the will to act. He can only accede to his catastrophe, and as he falls into the abyss,

> the world itself was bursting, bursting into black spouts of villages catapulted into space, with himself falling through it all, through

the inconceivable pandemonium of a million tanks, through the
blazing of ten million burning bodies, falling. . . .

(p. 375)

The Consul cannot organize his tragedy neatly into levels of
analogy; for him the analogies penetrate one another constantly.
At every turn he confronts an image of his tragic plight, and he
scarcely has a chance to react to one form of his perdition before
it metamorphoses, with frightening fluidity, into another equally
formidable. The same mental process which makes his back yard
into a fallen Eden transforms it as quickly into Elsinore, or
Munich. Since he always projects himself onto the world, he en-
counters his reflected image everywhere, variously distorted but
consistently foreboding. This pernicious interconnectedness is an
outgrowth of the Consul's reflexiveness; but his reflexiveness verges
on an aesthetic impulse which imbues his experience with the
beauty of formal coherence.

The Consul is engaged in a dizzying interchange: as his world
mirrors the image of himself, so he in turn mimics that reflected
image in his subsequent actions. "Mirror," "projection," "image"
—such tropes suggest delusion, and indeed, the Consul's confreres
find his obsessions phantasmal and unnecessary. Yet Lowry asserts
an idealism by whose standards the exasperated common sense of
Yvonne and Hugh is revealed as naïve and irrelevant. The Consul's
hallucinations substantiate such idealism; they are frighteningly,
palpably real. Lowry follows a favourite philosopher, Ortega, who
writes that "Appearance is an objective quality of the real";[22] and
he echoes Nietzsche in attributing to subjectivism a creative
agency—we *make* what we perceive. By extending this function in
time one arrives at Ortega's metaphor, which Lowry so admired,
of man as the novelist of himself.

But although man creates himself constantly, he lacks complete
artistic freedom. He can image himself only within the para-
meters of his experience; for as Ortega also suggests, "man is
'what has happened to him.' "[23] This tension between his dis-
quieting freedom to create himself anew at every moment, and his
subjugation to the dictates of his past, baffles the Consul's sense
of moral responsibility. When events ratify his tragic apprehen-
sions, he is incapable of determining whether those events are self-
fulfilling prophecies or confirmations of a transcendent necessity—

67

in other words, whether he is governed by internal or external necessity.[24]

Granted that the Consul's subjective interpretation of the world is real, in Ortega's sense, we may go a step further and conclude that his habit of interpreting and projecting fictions is in no way aberrant. Indeed, Lowry is careful to expose this habit in all the major characters; in each case their preoccupation with their fictions stands in the way of realizing them. Even what one may describe as harsh "realities" are inextricable from fiction-making: the action that objectifies the Consul's tragic projections—his murder by the fascists—results from the fiction that he is an anarchist spy.

Nevertheless, one can at least vary and privilege one's fictions. The Consul's subjectivism involves interpretation as well as projection, and in the former act his reflexiveness confers a blessing: it provides him with a critique of himself. For he is not only an obsessive reader of himself and his world; he is also a keen one, capable of seeing loopholes and interpreting himself quite dispassionately from the outside, as we might read him. At times the Consul is so critically aware of his fictions that he will puncture his own tragic rhetoric with a comic self-irony that is quite charming and humanizing. For while the Consul is an *alazon*, "an imposter in the sense that he is self-deceived or made dizzy by hubris",[25] he is also an ironist who occasionally reveals unexpected levels of self-knowledge and judgment. Yet the irony is not merely reductive; it works in both directions, finding some truth in both his postures and his self-mockery.

The Consul's problem is that this perspectivism holds him in suspension. Knowing his tragic identity to be at once authentic and delusory, he is paralysed—and through his paralysis the tragedy becomes authentic by default. Lowry himself cannot make up his mind about the dilemma. While he encourages the reader to sympathize with the Consul's internal constraints, he also seems to levy a judgment on his paralysis, particularly in the political context. Yet it is significant that the only model of selfless and fruitful striving, Juan Cerillo, is absent from the ruined garden. No character in the novel succeeds in pulling himself out of the subjective mire. Even when the Consul judges himself, facing death (the final critique of his paralysis), Lowry backs away from the judgment through the paradox of death as a "real abstraction":

> ... he had become ... the pilferer of meaningless muddled ideas out of which his rejection of life had grown, who had worn his two or three little bowler hats, his disguises, over these abstractions: now the realist of them all was close.
>
> (p. 374)

Yet out of this relativistic chaos, one incontrovertible truth emerges: that all the fictions are human fictions, with palpable effects on human joy and suffering. The Consul has steadily been driven by his past to pursue his future; his situation derives a mesmerizing unreality from the intense vertigo of defining himself in flux. When his fictions issue in praxis, when his spiritual tragedy becomes bodily, the Consul is taken by surprise: "Now he realized he had been shot. . . . 'Christ,' he remarked, puzzled, 'this is a dingy way to die.' " (p. 373).

Here the determining past at last collides with the projected future, and image and fact become one—the Consul is what he has become, and his reflexiveness falls away. This is his anagnorisis, "the recognition of the determined shape of the life he has created for himself . . . [and of] the uncreated life he has forsaken".[26] The Consul finally rejoins humanity, from which he has long alienated himself, in a community of suffering: ". . . someone had called him 'compañero' . . . It made him happy" (p. 374). His suffering also releases the Consul from the burden of moral judgment:

> Not that the truth is "bad" or "good": it simply *is*, is incomprehensible . . . being perpetually protean. Hence a final need probably for an acceptance of one's limitations, and of the absurd in oneself.[27]

Here is the afterglow of catharsis, a balm which Lowry felt compelled to provide. In most tragedies, a sense of inexorable movement toward a goal helps to relieve the suffering. The Consul's reflexiveness threatens that movement: instead of progress, we confront the dreadful possibility of an endless, meaningless shuttling between image and action. The Consul's death provides a momentary discharge of the tension into an event, a transitory pattern; yet the relief scarcely mitigates the claustrophobic terror of his reflexiveness.

NOTES

1 Douglas Day, *Malcolm Lowry: A Biography* (New York, 1973), pp. 299–326.

2 Malcolm Lowry, *Under the Volcano* (London, 1967), pp. 68–9. All subsequent page references to this text will be given in parentheses.

3 John Bunyan, *Grace Abounding* and *The Pilgrim's Progress*, ed. John Brown (Cambridge, 1907), p. 54.

4 Hugh later translates it properly: "Do you like this garden, the notice said, that is yours? See to it that your children do not destroy it!" (p. 232).

5 Tony Kilgallin points out that Lowry owned Burnet's *The Sacred Theory of the Earth*. See Kilgallin, *Lowry* (Erin, Ontario, 1973), p. 183.

6 Roma Gill, ed., Christopher Marlowe, *Doctor Faustus* (London, 1965), p. xxiv.

7 Malcolm Lowry, *Selected Letters of Malcolm Lowry*, ed. Harvey Breit and Margerie Bonner Lowry (London, 1967), p. 71.

8 *Ibid.*, p. 71.

9 Perle S. Epstein, *The Private Labyrinth of Malcolm Lowry: "Under the Volcano" and the Cabbala* (New York, 1969), p. 29.

10 *Ibid.*, p. 9.

11 See Northrop Frye, "The Drunken Boat," in *Romanticism Reconsidered: Selected Papers from the English Institute*, ed. Frye (New York, 1963), *passim*.

12 By mistaking the meaning of the Hebrew *Sod*, "secret", Lowry associates the abuse of wine with the ruined garden motif. See *Selected Letters*, p. 71.

13 "I believe that I am in hell, therefore I am." Arthur Rimbaud, "Une saison en enfer", in *Poesies, Une saison en enfer, et Illuminations*, ed. Louis Forestier (Paris, 1973), p. 132.

14 Epstein, p. 27.

15 "What holds the world together in its soul", Goethe, *Faust: Der Tragödie Erster Teil*, 11. 382–3.

16 Mann's *Doktor Faustus*, published in the same year as *Under the Volcano*, affords an interesting contrast: Leverkühn seeks salvation by striving unceasingly downward.

17 See *Selected Letters*, p. 84.

18 Lowry referred to *Under the Volcano* as the Inferno of a divine comedy including *Lunar Caustic* and the lost *In Ballast to the White Sea*. Yet he had virtually completed the first two of these novels by the time he concocted this grandiose scheme in 1940–41.

19 "I believe that the vulture is sweet to Prometheus and that the Ixions amuse themselves in hell."

20 The old fiddler stops to call him *"compañero"*, the rider's last word and, as Stephen Spender notes in his introduction to the novel (p. xxii), "the word of address used by the Reds in the Spanish Civil War".

21 *Selected Letters*, p. 79.

22 *Obras Completas* (Madrid, 1946), III, p. 236; trans. Claudio Guillén, *Literature as System: Essays Toward the Theory of Literary History* (Princeton, 1971), pp. 337–8.
23 *Selected Letters*, p. 210.
24 The difficulty of discriminating Self and World plagued Lowry, too, so that in many of his later novels and stories he fictionalized himself in a succession of personae, each of which is the ostensible author of Lowry's previous novel; and he always harboured the misgiving that he was himself being written.
25 Frye, *Anatomy of Criticism: Four Essays* (Princeton, 1971), p. 217.
26 *Ibid.*, p. 212.
27 Lowry, "Ghostkeeper", *American Review*, No. 17 (May 1973), p. 30.

3

Aspects of Language in
Under the Volcano

by BRIAN O'KILL

"If Mr. Lowry would sieve out his style a bit, and prune the abandoned, brilliant image, I think he would be . . . an outstanding
writer."[1] So wrote one of the original reviewers of *Under the
Volcano* in 1947, and an easy scornful reply is not justified merely
by hindsight and Lowry's fairly steady reputation. Since recent
studies of his work continue to hint at some uneasiness about his
use of language, we are still faced with the implication that the
language of *Under the Volcano* is an optional decorative element
which could be sieved, pruned, or otherwise altered without shak-
ing the work's foundations. This is, I think, a fallacious reason for
a valid line of inquiry; for better or worse, Lowry's characteristic
methods of verbal organization are very closely related to the total
construction and coherence of the novel.

Lowry was only too ready to anticipate adverse judgments on
almost every point of his immensely laboured and self-conscious
novel, and in his anxiously jocular preface to a French edition he
pretended to admit that his style bore "an embarrassing resemblance to that of the German writer Schopenhauer describes, who
wished to express six things at the same time instead of discussing them one after the other. 'In those long, rich parenthetical
periods, like boxes enclosing boxes, and crammed more full than
roast geese stuffed with apples, one's memory above all is put to
the task, when understanding and judgment should have been
called upon to do their work.' "[2] Within *Under the Volcano* one
can find comparable phrases providing, according to the author,
"a suggestion that the book was satirizing itself".[3] Thus, within a
Mexican tourist-guide which offers an ironic perversion of the Eng-

lish language, there are references to "a churrigueresque (overloaded) style", "overloaded art work", "an overloading style", "an
overloaded and embellished style".[4] Another revealing image of
Lowry's attitude to his work is suggested by his protagonist's
reaction to an overgrown garden: "Oddly enough, it did not strike
him as being nearly so 'ruined' as it had earlier appeared. Such
chaos as might exist even lent an added charm. He liked the exuberance of the unclipped growth at hand" (pp. 127–8).

The "unclipped growth" and the attempt "to express six things
at the same time" are concomitant features of the novel which
largely account for its language and form. As an initial specimen
of Lowry's method, here is a fairly typical sentence from the opening chapter: Jacques Laruelle, a French ex-film-director, walks
(in a circle, as Lowry's characters usually move and think) around
the Mexican town of Quauhnahuac, ruminating upon, among other
things, his desire for the deceased wife of his deceased friend
Geoffrey Firmin:

> His passion for Yvonne (whether or not she'd ever been much
> good as an actress was beside the point, he'd told her the truth
> when he said she would have been more than good in any film
> he made) had brought back to his heart, in a way he could not
> have explained, the first time that alone, walking over the meadows
> from Saint Près, the sleepy French village of backwaters and
> locks and grey disused watermills where he was lodging, he had
> seen, rising slowly and wonderfully and with boundless beauty
> above the stubble fields blowing with wildflowers, slowly rising
> into the sunlight, as centuries before the pilgrims straying over
> those same fields had watched them rise, the twin spires of
> Chartres Cathedral.
>
> (p. 12)

The most marked and characteristic feature of this sentence
is the use of self-embedding clauses interrupting the main syntactical movement. The basic statement is split into five isolated
sections: "His passion for Yvonne / had brought back to his
heart / the first time that alone / he had seen / the twin spires
of Chartres Cathedral." Between each unit and its successor there
is at least one intervening modification: a parenthetical disjunct,
participle clauses premodifying subject and object, an appositive
noun-phrase, and adverbial, relative and comparative clauses. Thus
four-fifths of the sentence, 100 words out of 124, consists of

grammatically peripheral material, of elaborations and qualifications inserted into the framework at almost every possible point. These frequent interruptions have an effect, on one level, of mimicking the hesitations and divagations of spontaneous mental activity; but there are also larger authorial intentions at stake. Lowry seems to avoid, for as long as possible, finishing and defining the sentence as a unit: through the withholding of the grammatical resolution until the very end of the sentence, all the elements are kept in fluid suspension until the last; the middle of the sentence is held together not by strong syntactical organization but by the non-committal verbal repetition of "rising slowly . . . slowly rising . . . rise". Such a suspension and recapitulation of syntax, necessitating repetition of a key word after a number of modifiers have disrupted the basic structure, is not an uncommon feature in Lowry's work. Peripheral material often seems to acquire so much weight and momentum of its own that it threatens to destroy the shape and coherence of a sentence—just as, on first or on tenth reading, the main structures of the novel may seem to be obscured by so much material of little apparent relevance.

On closer examination, however, the main digression in this sentence is seen to make a fairly important contribution. No doubt it is a manifestation of Lowry's restless habit of sticking every possible fragment of his experience into his work, however tangential it may seem to his immediate purposes; it must have been in 1933 or 1934 that he himself first visited Chartres, and ten years later he suddenly inserted the material into the middle of a description of Mexican landscape. But the digression is probably not irrelevant to his broader intentions. The opening paragraph of *Under the Volcano*, symbolically locating Quauhnahuac at the heart of the world, signals clearly enough that he is attempting to write not just about a few mediocre people in a particular locality at a specific period of history, but also about universal human history and consciousness. If the characters of the novel are presented as symptomatic of universal processes, it is also true that universality exists within them. It is quite characteristic that, within a sentence describing the thoughts of a modern man in Mexico, the reader is given a brief picture of medieval pilgrims, offering a glimpse of another time, another place, almost of another world. Within Lowry's ramifications, Mexico can be transformed into "every sort of landscape at once" (p. 10); within the inclusive

74

consciousness created in the novel, all kinds of disparate facts and feelings can be piled together, briefly illuminated by juxtaposition if not by any defined relationship. Syntactical digression and expansion might therefore be seen as one of the chief devices by which Lowry tries to merge specific and universal references.

As a further example, here is a sentence from the opening pages of the second chapter, narrating the moment of Yvonne Firmin's return to the town in which she left her husband a year previously:

> Ashamed, numb with nostalgia and anxiety, reluctant to enter the crowded bar, though equally reluctant to have the taxidriver go in for her, Yvonne, her consciousness so lashed by wind and air and voyage she still seemed to be travelling, still sailing into Acapulco harbour yesterday evening through a hurricane of immense and gorgeous butterflies swooping seaward to greet the *Pennsylvania*—at first it was as though fountains of multicoloured stationery were being swept out of the saloon lounge—glanced defensively round the square, really tranquil in the midst of this commotion, of the butterflies still zigzagging overhead or past the heavy open ports, endlessly vanishing astern, *their* square, motionless and brilliant in the seven o'clock morning sunlight, silent yet somehow poised, expectant, with one eye half open already, the merry-go-rounds, the Ferris wheel, lightly dreaming, looking forward to the fiesta later—the ranged rugged taxis too that were looking forward to something else, a taxi strike that afternoon, she'd been confidentially informed.
>
> (pp. 43–4)

When Albert Erskine, editor for Lowry's American publishers, objected that this sentence was "pretty difficult to come to grips with simply on account of its syntax and might be more effective if clarified", the author was quick to insist that "the overlapping style at this point is necessary".[5] At least Lowry did not seek to abrogate his authorial responsibility by claiming here that this is "Yvonne's style", a variety of language dictated by the character at the centre of the experience. These verbal torrents are not confined to Yvonne, and it would be easy to exaggerate the effect of the novel's shifting viewpoint upon its language. Although most of the novel is ostensibly mediated through the minds of its characters—each chapter through the consciousness of one of the four chief personages, whose viewpoint is explicitly established at the outset—this device is not maintained with inflexible consistency and is not a rigorously determining influence upon the novel's narrative and stylistic system. It was not established at all until a fairly late draft (ca. 1942), and in successive drafts the viewpoints of several chapters continued to change (thus Chapter IX, as Lowry admitted, passed from Hugh to Geoffrey to Yvonne);[6] from Lowry's manuscripts one can see that these changes did not modify the language to any great extent, because complete ventriloquism was never attempted. Lowry makes a few gestures towards varying the style, especially at the beginnings of chapters, and the specific content of a chapter may impose some superficial distinctiveness; but detailed and quantitative analysis of various features serves only to show that there is little objective linguistic basis for distinguishing one chapter from another. The usual effects of shifting multipersonal viewpoint in fiction—interpretation of data from different angles, irony arising from a character's partial apprehension of a situation, stylistic contrasts—are not Lowry's real aim. His method of characterization, according to his own account, is one of "heteroplasty",[7] in which the four chief persons are intended to be "aspects of the same man, or of the human spirit";[8] his object is to create a composite, inclusive or collective consciousness with unlimited resources of learning, memory, and language.

In describing the complicated structure of this sentence, it would be more precise to call it "branching" or "cumulative" than to use Lowry's term "overlapping". It is not built on a traditional hypotactic Ciceronian pattern, with carefully arranged subordination, strongly connected members, emphatic antithesis and parallelism, and with all elements clearly related to a central or climactic clause. My diagram of the main elements is an attempt to emphasize the amorphous sequence of ramifying loosely-linked units, some of them hanging almost in mid-air. The main clause (items 5 and 10) is of little intrinsic importance, but the sentence clusters around it in three large branches (left-, mid-, and right-branches) which in turn lead to numerous other ramifications. Most of these are, grammatically speaking, "free" or "non-restrictive" modifiers: elements which are not strictly necessary for the definition or linguistic completion of the unit from which they arise, but which can be added or subtracted by the writer at will.

To begin with, there is a long left-branching construction composed of four adjectival phrases (1–4; the fourth is actually subordinate to the third). Thus the main statement, the subject of the sentence, is deliberately withheld; and the belated appearance

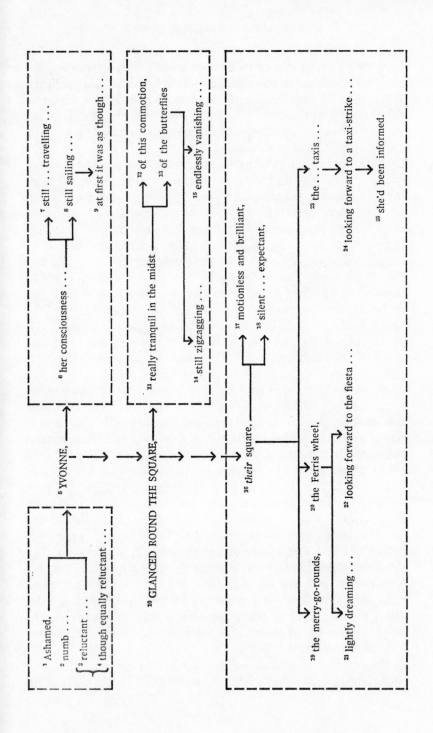

¹ Ashamed,
² numb . . . .
³ reluctant . . .
⁴ though equally reluctant . . .

⁵ YVONNE,

⁶ her consciousness . . . .

⁷ still . . . travelling . . . .
⁸ still sailing . . .
⁹ at first it was as though . . . .

¹⁰ GLANCED ROUND THE SQUARE,

¹¹ really tranquil in the midst

¹² of this commotion,
¹³ of the butterflies

¹⁴ still zigzagging . . .

¹⁵ endlessly vanishing . . .

¹⁶ *their* square,

¹⁷ motionless and brilliant,
¹⁸ silent . . . expectant,

¹⁹ the merry-go-rounds,

²⁰ the Ferris wheel,

²¹ lightly dreaming . . . .

²² looking forward to the fiesta . . .

²³ the . . . taxis . . .

²⁴ looking forward to a taxi-strike . . . .

²⁵ she'd been informed.

of Yvonne in the sentence strikes me as an apt reflection of her hesitation and reluctance to disclose herself. Moreover, the position of the subject in the sentence—detached from the predicate, surrounded by vast modifications—may be taken as an image of the character in the middle of the square, or in the middle of her life, overwhelmed by all the circumstances surrounding her, detached even from her own actions.

After the subject (5), the sentence goes into a mid-branching or self-embedding modification, with an absolute clause (6) leading to a further subordinate element which, without any break of syntactical continuity, totally alters the topic: it moves from "today" to "yesterday", from Quauhnahuac to Acapulco, from land to sea (7–9). This ramification leads so far away from the base that the appearance of the predicate (10) is abrupt and almost confusing; but at this point the main grammatical structure ceases, and the sentence runs away in a long amorphous right-branch consisting mainly of noun phrases appositive to "the square". The noun is first modified by an adjectival phrase (11), which bifurcates (12–13), with the second fork splitting again into two parallel phrases (14–15). The noun is then repeated appositively in a specified emphatic form (16), and modified again by two asymmetric adjectival phrases (17–18), before it is particularized by three more appositive nouns (19, 20, 23) detailing its components, two of which lead to further branches (21–2, 24–5). Such a process of continual adding and detailing, of moving away from general statement in a series of right-branching structures, is typical of Lowry's sentences, and it bears implications about his strategy in the novel. The "logic" is deductive rather than inductive, with a movement away from generalized definition towards illustrative detail; the structure is expansive, avoiding the closed unit of the periodic sentence in favour of an open form with an almost infinite capacity for addition and reduplication. It is clear, too, that this centrifugal development shows a dangerous tendency towards formlessness and lack of definition: this sentence displays some awkwardness and loss of momentum in the final phrases (24–5), and it is noticeable how often Lowry's sentences drift away into an indeterminate ellipsis, seeming to conclude only because the author had run out of breath or ideas.

The amount of matter compressed within the limits of this single sentence is, nonetheless, remarkable. Of course there is no way of actually saying six things at once in language; but if we take the sentence-unit as a metaphorical equivalent of a single moment of time, we can see that Lowry's language mimics a kind of simultaneity. Within his branching syntax the past is merged almost imperceptibly into the present, apparently imputing to the present scene a quality ("this commotion", referring not to Quauhnahuac but to Acapulco) existing only in the memory. That is not all, for two other time-schemes are implicit: the previous year, suggested by the phrase "*their* square" which evokes an old experience shared by Yvonne and her husband, and the future, implied by the repeated phrase "looking forward". Thus four scenes are coalesced; each subtly flows into each, within the loose framework of the sentence.

There is a suggestive phrase, attributed to Bergson, in Lowry's essay "Garden of Etla": "The sense of time is an inhibition to prevent everything happening at once."[9] Lowry's conceptions of time were also evidently influenced by the serialist theories of J. W. Dunne, whose *An Experiment with Time* (published in 1927) posited the existence of "absolute time" containing all moments of past, present, and future; and some of Lowry's long sentences do seem to create a kind of "absolute time", an interminable continuum in which everything can happen at once. His aim was in fact very similar to that of William Faulkner (of whom I shall have more to say at a later point), as quoted by Malcolm Cowley: " 'My ambition,' he said, 'is to put everything into one sentence— not only the present but the whole past on which it depends and which keeps overtaking the present, second by second.' He went on to explain that in writing his prodigious sentences he is trying to convey a sense of simultaneity, not only giving what happened in the shifting moment but suggesting everything that went before and made the quality of that moment."[10]

This attempt is reinforced by one of the most distinctive verbal features of Lowry's prose: his use of adjectival accumulation in long pre-modification sequences, such as "the swift leathery perfumed alcoholic dusk" (p. 45), "her guilty divorced dead helplessness" (p. 265), and "a black lateral abstract sky" (p. 83). In *Under the Volcano* there are about a hundred instances of such series of three or more attributive adjectives arranged without punctuation or co-ordination, and although the device was probably taken over by Lowry from Faulkner (there are no less than five examples in the opening sentence of *Absalom, Absalom!*, published in 1936,[11] its function in his work is quite revealing.

It is true that in some of these sequences there is not much more than tautologous synonymy. Lowry was no believer in the single *mot juste*, and would not willingly use one word where six were possible; nor would he have subscribed to the traditional doctrine of teachers of composition that adjectives should be used sparingly and subordinated to strong concrete nouns. To his way of thinking, the bare name of something was a restrictive over-simplification, and a thing could only be defined—or encompassed, at least—as the sum of all its perceived attributes. But although he may not have seen life steadily, somehow he did try to see it whole. In some of his descriptive phrases there is an effective compression of minute, and seemingly disparate, details into a single brief sequence. Unexpected collocations of adjectives are produced; there is a fusion of an unusual mixture of sensory impressions, as in "the swift leathery perfumed alcoholic dusk", or of objective description and impressionistic reactions, as in "the black lateral abstract sky", or of paradoxical attributes, as in "the numb brilliant jittering city" (p. 265). The suggestion of seeing an object from a number of different angles is linked to an effect of unity and simultaneity produced by the lack of punctuation and co-ordinators. A phrase like "sudden intoxicating terrified incidence" (p. 100) evokes a different response from, say, "sudden, intoxicating, and terrified incidence"; in the latter, there is a pause over each epithet separately, while in the former each adjective is presented not as a discrete modifier of the noun but as part of a cumulative sequence. Hence emphasis falls not on the individual detail but on the series as a whole; the description is not analytic but synthetic, intending to recombine the fragments of hurried perception into a momentary apprehension of the wholeness and complexity of an experience.

Frequent and original similes are another characteristic of Lowry's prose; in particular, it is the isolated comic or incongruous comparison which he uses with so much exuberance and imagination. (The device can be traced right back to stories he wrote as a schoolboy, in which—probably under the influence of P. G. Wodehouse and other popular contemporary writers—he threw off such phrases as "a peculiarly scaly radiator which exuded about as much heat as a polar bear with frostbite."[12] Later influences upon his use of similes probably include Gogol and Faulkner.) In these, any object and ground of comparison seem possible: "Darkness had fallen like the House of Usher" (p. 22); "the Consul, innocently as a man who has committed a murder while dummy at bridge, entered Yvonne's room" (p. 81); "white sculpturings of clouds, like a billowing concept in the brain of Michelangelo" (p. 118); "curious agonized whines, or provocative nocturnal meows, like a nightmare in the soul of George Frederic Watts" (p. 155). In each example the disparity between the tenor and vehicle of comparison is striking, and perhaps on occasion the conceit is excessively artificial; yet this incongruity is characteristic of Lowry's method. He is not greatly concerned to maintain strict consistency of character, verisimilitude, or tone; he is willing to puncture the dramatic illusion, so that the reader has to "believe and not believe and then again to believe";[13] he couples the grandiose and tragic with the commonplace and absurd, the immediacy of dramatic situation with the detachment of aesthetic contemplation. By yoking together heterogeneous concepts he gives himself freedom to incorporate tangential literary allusions, hints of wider perspectives, glimpses of other worlds outside the immediate Mexican scene or even almost outside the consciousness of his characters. The fairly common nautical imagery, for instance, while having some specific dramatic function (providing an image of escape, cleansing and purification, and offering resonant contrasts between water and alcohol, between the open ocean and the land-locked torrid Mexican terrain), is also an interesting symptom of Lowry's attempt to encompass the widest possible range of implied experience in the novel: the nautical images invoke a whole milieu outside the basic naturalistic setting, and compose a kind of "other landscape" (to use the phrase of Alain-Fournier, whose Le Grand Meaulnes has a rather similar series of images).[14] The centrifugal movement of all these images is perhaps correspondent to the many evocations of flight and escape in the novel—the release of a trapped seagull or a caged eagle, Yvonne's dream of escape from Mexico to Canada, the flight of her spirit towards the stars, the ascent of the volcano; the aim is to get away from the dinginess and muddle of immediate reality, with all its prosaic obligations, and to take refuge in the spiritual worlds of other artists and writers, in witty nonsense, or even in just a simple innocent domestic pastime like a game of cards.

Lowry's fondness for the lengthy and striking simile—a device now fallen into rather unjustified disrepute among serious writers —tells us something more about his strategy. In comparison with a metaphor, a simile is both more explicit and more tentative. A metaphor is linguistically indistinguishable from literal statement, whereas a simile is always marked by a formal phrase of comparison, "like" or "as"; yet whereas metaphor is a covert assertion of identity between two elements, the simile retains an open or tentative quality, being merely a suggestion of potential similarity—A is related to B at some point, it tells us, but no more. This vague suggestiveness of the simile suited Lowry, who might well be described as an analogist rather than a symbolist; his profuse novel resists attempts to reduce its concrete properties to definite abstractions. Although early drafts of *Under the Volcano* were crammed with portentous small generalizations, most of these were weeded out before publication as his ambitions grew increasingly large and ill-defined. Where they survive, in such similes as "Hugh regarded his cigarette that seemed bent, like humanity, on consuming itself as quickly as possible" (p. 101), the effect is deplorable more because of the weakness of the insight than because of the clumsy but well-meaning attempt at definition. Lowry's usual method, on the contrary, is to illustrate an impalpable entity in concrete terms: "an agony chill as that iced mescal drunk in the Hotel Canada on the morning of Yvonne's departure" (p. 129); he shuns definition and intellectual simplification in favour of undefined images and correspondences, *"ayant l'expansion des choses infinies"*.

This incurable habit of analogy is built into the character of the novel's protagonist (see, for example, Firmin's ruminations in the Salón Ofélia on p. 287). "There is no explanation of my life" (p. 289), Geoffrey Firmin says—or boasts, for he will cursorily reject any explanation offered to him. This is perhaps the very reason for his inability to grasp the simplest facts of his existence: the chaos in his mind arises less from a vision of universal disorder than from excess of a kind of delusive order created by a baffling plethora of correspondences. Everything, to his mind, appears to be related to something else; therefore nothing *is*, clearly, simply, and uniquely. "To discover correspondences in the world around us," notes Gabriel Josipovici, "does not lead to the sensation that we are inhabiting a meaningful universe; on the contrary, it leads to the feeling that what we had taken to be 'the world' is only the projection of our private compulsions: *analogy* becomes a sign of *dementia*."[15]

Lowry's way of thinking is betrayed by his fondness for occult or pseudo-philosophical systems depicting the universe as an ever-expanding organism based around some indefinable *primum mobile*. He was impressed by the misty works of P. D. Ouspensky, with their emphasis on the unity of all human activity; by Hermann Keyserling's *Recovery of Truth*, from which he copied out such commonplaces as "There live in every man, in some stratum of his being, all conceivable types of man";[16] by Annie Besant's description of the Great Tao which "has no name but it effects the growth and maintenance of all things";[17] by Charles Fort, who conceived of the universe as "one inter-continuous nexus, in which and of which all seeming things are only different expressions",[18] and whose pell-mell writings show all too clearly his contempt for scientific classification and logical analysis; by Charles Stansfeld-Jones' eccentric neo-Cabbalism, in which life is depicted as a branching tree or a series of artificially connected spheres.[19] Probably this disreputable intellectual background taught Lowry nothing new, but it gave him a spurious authority for the indiscriminate attitude towards phenomena which is so marked in even his best work.

In his later novel *Dark as the Grave Wherein My Friend Is Laid*, speaking through the novelist Sigbjørn Wilderness, Lowry sought to defend himself against criticism that he tried "to get too much in" his works. Wilderness argues that "it's better to get too much in than to get too little out," and adds: "Part of the artist's despair . . . in the face of his material is perhaps occasioned by the patent fact that the universe itself—as the Rosicrucians also held—is in the process of creation. An organic work of art, having been conceived, must grow in the creator's mind, or proceed to perish."[20] All very well, but the *artist* has to find a beginning and end to this process, and it is an apparent failure on this score which has led to the common criticism of *Under the Volcano* that it is excessively inflated by laboured accretion of material. I do not think that the criticism can be answered simply by saying that such criteria had no place in Lowry's aesthetic; but perhaps it is possible to show, by a brief examination of the linguistic evolution of the novel, that there was some genuine internal dynamism which produced the "overloaded style". Consider, for example, the opening of Chapter III in the version of the novel which Lowry unsuccessfully submitted for publication in 1940. Here Geoffrey Firmin's daughter Yvonne has just entered Quauhnahuac with her friend Hugh Fernhead (I doubt whether Lowry intended the name to mean "feather-brain", but it is appropriate); the passage corresponds to pp. 43–5 of Chapter II of the published version, including the long sentence I have previously quoted:

> They walked down a little hill and almost immediately were in the square. A long paper poster strung from tree to tree said: "*Hotel Bella Vista Gran Baile a Beneficio de la Crux Roja. Los Mejores artistas del radio en accion.*"
>
> Preparation was evidently being made for a fiesta. They passed a Ferris wheel, booths, a merry go round. From the Bella Vista Hotel issued weary music; the ball seemed to be still going on. Stragglers passed them, returning home, looking white and exhausted in the morning light. . . .
>
> They went into the Bella Vista and inquired at the lobby. But at the mention of her father's name the clerk, with an amiable smile, pointed to the bar. They entered the bar, blinking in the dusk after the pulsing light, and Yvonne felt her soul contract, as though a car with locked wheels had suddenly skidded to rest in gravel behind her.

In many ways the 1940 version is almost unrecognizably different from the final text; yet the main reason for the difference is not a radical change of the basic linguistic and stylistic structures but a process of vast growth and shift and emphasis. The early version shows in fact the very basis of Lowry's prose, as it was formed during the 1930s in his various drafts of *Lunar Caustic* and in such stories as "June 30th 1934!".[21] In these works a restricted plain style predominates: brief declarative sentences, usually composed of a single finite clause; a deliberate lack of connexion between sentences and clauses, with frequent use of asyndeton (omission of co-ordinators) and "run-on" constructions (unco-ordinated juxtaposition of independent clauses with different subjects); adjectives used sparingly, and most often singly; fairly basic vocabulary; infrequent use of similes and rhetorical figures.

Lowry was always very vulnerable to the influence of other writers. Probably the single most potent influence upon his language during the 1930s was the English translation of Nordahl Grieg's unremarkable novel *The Ship Sails On*;[22] but there were also more widespread tendencies among writers of this period to which he conformed. At a time when some of the most vociferous critics and novelists among Lowry's contemporaries were advocating the necessity for topical, objective and austere writing, his friend Arthur Calder-Marshall was demanding that "the writer must redeem common speech from loose phrase and thought. His language must be clear, precise and economical."[23] These self-imposed restrictions may not have been intrinsically wrong; within them flourished a few admirable writers using language more precisely and economically than Lowry could ever do, masters of understatement, of drawing their effects from a deliberately circumscribed range of linguistic resources, distrustful of big words and florid structures. Yet at worst these methods could degenerate into a common twilight greyness and lack of individuality, which Cyril Connolly ingeniously demonstrated by concocting a passage from separate sentences by Isherwood, Hemingway, and Orwell in which hardly any stylistic inconsistency was visible.[24] In Lowry's case, his talent lay in other directions: so that, just as his echoing of the fashions of Leftist politics in the 1930s is quite unconvincing, so his efforts to ape these stylistic procedures resulted all too often in sheer monotony.

It would be natural to expect the earlier version of *Under the Volcano* to be more subjective or autobiographical, less organized and coherent, than the final text. In fact it is boringly objective and restrained: a plodding narrative, devoid of linguistic or mental vitality, offering a detached, passive and fragmentary vision of the world. The minimal syntax gives no room for manœuvre or involvement; it just presents the facts relentlessly, moment by moment, one at a time, without connexion or focus of consciousness. In comparison with this text—or with Lowry's rather halting attempts to achieve simplicity in such later works as "The Forest Path to the Spring"—the real virtues of the language of *Under the Volcano* stand out; for it is superior not only in vitality and expressiveness, but even in compression and elegance.

When Lowry began to rewrite the novel in 1941, he must soon have realized that greater linguistic resources were needed. "Not so many paragraphs" he scrawled twice in the margin of the first page of the old draft, thus suggesting his awareness of the need to connect isolated fragments into larger coherent units. By 1942 or 1943 Yvonne's arrival in Quauhnahuac had taken this shape:

> Ashamed, hesitant, numbly excited, Yvonne was gazing defensively around the square, "their" square, brilliant in the seven o'clock morning sunlight, silent yet poised, expectant, looking forward to the fiesta later, the booths shut up, but with one eye open already, the merry-go-rounds only half asleep, the Ferris wheel dreaming—the ranged, rugged, taxis too, that were looking forward to something else their default at the airport perhaps presaged, a strike that afternoon she'd just been confidentially informed.

Compared with this draft, the final version of the passage shows a slight amount of rearrangement (the phrase "looking forward to the fiesta later" is postponed), a couple of simple word-for-word alterations (e.g. "glanced" for "was gazing"), three small deletions ("the booths shut up", "only half asleep", "their default . . . presaged"), and, above all, numerous additions. There are some typical modifying enlargements, mainly of adverbs and adjectives —thus "brilliant" becomes "motionless and brilliant", "dreaming" becomes "lightly dreaming", and so on; but in particular there is considerable expansion caused by the introduction of new material. Yvonne's arrival in Acapulco, which in earlier drafts had been described separately in an earlier chapter, is thrust into the middle of the sentence, yet without altering its basic construction; and if we consider how many elements Lowry gradually added to his text in this way, we can see how the characteristic form of his long sentences evolved. Additional information, descriptive details, tangential analogies, literary allusions, fusions of past and future time with the present: as all these were loosely inserted into the simple basic structure, so the flexible cumulative sentence, swollen with modification and parenthesis, took shape.

This large stylistic change has to be seen both as a cause and as an effect of Lowry's widening conception of the novel. The language grew more complex because of the way that Lowry added new material, draft by draft; at the same time, this expansion was made possible only by the development of an adaptable stylistic system. Among the external reasons for this development, I think that the stylistic influence of William Faulkner is outstanding; and that, appropriately, this influence may have reached Lowry through the intervention of his former mentor Conrad Aiken. Although in a letter of 1940 Lowry made a slightly caustic reference to Faulkner's novels being "full of . . . poems",[25] in later years he made a number of admiring comments on his work, and on two occasions in 1946 voluntarily acknowledged some echoes of Faulkner in *Under the Volcano*.[26] In 1939 Aiken published a stimulating essay exploring the correspondence of linguistic and narrative structures in Faulkner's work; according to his autobiography *Ushant*, he began work on this piece while staying with Lowry in Mexico in 1937,[27] so it is more than possible that at this time he planted in Lowry's mind certain notions of the potential expressiveness of syntax which were later to blossom in *Under the Volcano*. After some preliminary exasperated jibes at Faulkner's "strangely fluid and slippery and heavily mannered prose", much of what Aiken says about Faulkner is so equally applicable to Lowry that it deserves to be quoted at some length:

> Overelaborate they certainly are, baroque and involuted in the extreme, these sentences: trailing clauses, one after another, shadowily in apposition, or perhaps not even with so much connection as that; parenthesis after parenthesis, the parenthesis itself often containing one or more parentheses . . . It is as if Mr. Faulkner, in a sort of hurried despair, had decided to try to tell us everything, absolutely everything, every last origin or source or quality or qualification, and every possible future or permutation as well, in one terrifically concentrated effort: each sentence to be, as it were, a microcosm. . . .
>
> Nevertheless . . . if one considers these queer sentences not simply by themselves, as monsters of grammar or awkwardness, but in their relation to the book as a whole, one sees a functional reason and necessity for their being as they are. . . . It is a persistent offering of obstacles, a calculated system of screens and obtrusions, of confusions and ambiguous interpolations and delays, with one express purpose; and that purpose is simply to keep the form—and the idea—fluid and unfinished, still in motion, as it were, and unknown, until the dropping into place of the very last syllable. . . .
>
> What Mr. Faulkner is after, in a sense, is a *continuum*. He wants a medium without stops or pauses, a medium which is always *of the moment*, and of which the passage from moment to moment is as fluid and undetectable as in the life itself which he is purporting to give. It is all inside and underneath, or as seen

from within and below; the reader must therefore be steadily *drawn in*; he must be powerfully and unremittingly hypnotized inward and downward to that image-stream; and this suggests, perhaps, a reason not only for the length and elaborateness of the sentence structure, but for the repetitiveness as well.[28]

It was Aiken, too, who saluted Lowry on the dust-wrapper of the first American edition of *Under the Volcano*: "Let us all give humble and grateful thanks that we can once again, after a long walk in the desert of contemporary prose, salute a novelist who can really *write*. Malcolm Lowry's *Under the Volcano* must be, for anyone who loves the English language, a sheer joy." Aiken does well to remind us that Lowry's linguistic resourcefulness can be, at best, one of the chief aesthetic pleasures of the novel. That should not imply that Lowry is a particularly grandiose or precious writer —the rather inflationary tendency of his polysyllabic adjectives and emotionally-freighted abstract nouns is often offset by colloquial turns of phrase and loose syntax; nor that his language is without humane purpose. Since the value attached to language by an author may be an index of his judgment of the subject, Lowry's devotion of lavish resources of language to his work is a memorial to his characters, an assertion of belief, an evocation of times "when an individual life held some value and was not a mere misprint in a communiqué" (p. 5).

Throughout *Under the Volcano* there are, nonetheless, signs of an ambivalent attitude towards language. In so far as it is a part or symptom of a civilization which is shown to be on the verge of disintegration, language itself is imperilled. The incomprehensible utterances of foreigners, drunks, and illiterates threaten a breakdown of human communication; in Mexico, so Geoffrey Firmin insisted, was "the original Tower of Babel" (p. 11), and the last chapter of the novel is an explicit vision of "the Babel . . . the confusion of tongues" (p. 366). Elsewhere, as in several of Lowry's other works, unsuccessful telephone calls provide images of failed and frustrated communication. Even between intimate people, language fails; in conversations between the main characters, true feelings are unexpressed and there is only silence, or laconic oblique statements, or pointless jaunty comments about the weather and other impersonal topics.

In another way, the cumulative effect of Lowry's constant use of linguistic approximators and diminishers is an implication of scepticism about the reality of language. The recurrence of such phrases as "in a way", "kind of", "as if", "almost", "somehow", indicates a retreat from clear defining statements; it is no wonder that "inexpressible", "indescribable" and "inenarrable" are among Lowry's favourite adjectives. With all these escape clauses, his work can be inordinately elusive, seeming to shun any firm commitment to anything in particular. Certainly in some of his writings after *Under the Volcano* his mania for qualification becomes like a nervous tic, attenuating the reality of the work and suggesting a failure of nerve in questions of selection and organization.

There is a curious method by which Lowry does demonstrate a very direct relationship between language and reality: words, in *Under the Volcano*, can sometimes be metamorphosed into actualities. A simile in which the vehicle of comparison seems incidental, "the tragic word droned round the room like a bullet that had passed through him" (p. 346), adumbrates the Consul's death by a real bullet; similarly, an image in the middle of the novel, "he crashed on through the metamorphoses of dying and reborn hallucinations, like a man who does not know he has been shot from behind" (p. 126), is clearly echoed at the moment of his death: "Now he realized he had been shot" (p. 373). The opening chapter contains a fanciful description of the Consul's handwriting, "the t's like lonely wayside crosses save where they crucified an entire word" (p. 35); in Chapter VII appears "a stone wayside cross" beside which a man lies in an attitude of crucifixion (p. 241). Thus the image is hypostasized; the figurative is merged with the literal; the "other landscape" glimpsed in Lowry's similes is fused into the setting of the novel.

If this imputes a magical quality to language, recalling primeval beliefs in the power of names to invoke the objects they represent, perhaps it need not be taken too seriously. But there is no doubt that Lowry saw language as a creative instrument rather than just as a tool for describing existing realities. Again I am reminded of a passage in one of Aiken's critical essays (a review of Nicolas Kostyleff's *Le mécanisme cérébrale de la pensée*): "By far the greater part of any poem is generated in the act of composition: as M. Kostyleff remarks, the initial stimulus, the stimulus which first set the language habit to work, is soon lost sight of in the wealth of other language associations which are evoked from the subconscious."[29] Or one could say that, in Lowry's case, the initial "action" of language provokes a prodigious "reaction", as the introductory approach towards an idea generates qualification, analogy, parallel, and so on. It is better to accept the element of arbitrariness in this process, as a consequence of the unique and dangerous freedom of fiction, than to find ingenious explanations. Given that the novel, although undeniably containing mimetic elements, is fundamentally a verbal construction based on nothing outside the writer's mind, it is questionable whether there are any reliable criteria, except a rationalization of our own experience of reading, by which we can judge whether Lowry "put too much in".

I suspect that Lowry's explicatory letter to Jonathan Cape—the basis for nearly all commentaries in the decade since its publication—has exercised a mischievous influence on some counts. On one hand, Lowry keeps reiterating that "all that is there is there for a reason"; but the attempt to justify every minutest element of the novel as an essential part of a unified master-plan was really a delusion. By 1949 Lowry had obviously changed his mind about this, since he expressed enthusiasm at the prospect of preparing an abridged version of the novel with large excisions of "some muddy Lowromancings".[30] On the other hand, in his insistence upon "deeper meanings" he allows that we may find "anything else we please" in the novel, and that "meanings" . . . are practically inexhaustible". He wishes "to hint that, as Henry James says, 'There are depths' "; but it may not be unfair to suggest that at times there are mere hints at undefined significance. If Lowry could quote Henry James to his purpose, one is tempted to reply with James' comment on Walt Whitman: "It is not enough to disregard everything in particular and to accept everything in general . . . to discharge the undigested contents of your blotting-book into the lap of the public."

NOTES

1   Elizabeth Johnson, *Commonweal*, 7 March 1947, p. 523.
2   "Preface to a Novel", in *Malcolm Lowry: The Man and His Work*, ed. George Woodcock (Vancouver, 1971), p. 9. This is Woodcock's re-translation of the preface to *Au-dessous du volcan* (Paris, 1949).
3   Letter to Jonathan Cape, January 1946: *Selected Letters of Malcolm Lowry* (London, 1967), p. 82.

4   *Under the Volcano* (New York, 1947), pp. 298–9. In all subsequent quotations from the novel, page numbers will be indicated in parentheses within the text.

5   Unpublished correspondence between Lowry and Erskine, 14 and 22 June 1946, preserved among the Lowry papers in the library of the University of British Columbia.

6   Letter to Cape: *Selected Letters*, p. 79.

7   Lowry used this term in a review of Earle Birney's novel *Turvey*, suggesting that "All the Canadian characters, bad or good as they happen to be, all seem to add up to Turvey": *Thunderbird*, 5 (December 1947), p. 27.

8   Letter to Cape: *Selected Letters*, p. 60.

9   *United Nations World*, 4 (June 1950), p. 47.

10 *The Faulkner/Cowley File* (London, 1966), p. 112.

11 Henry James, whose stylistic influence is certainly evident in the middle three stories of Lowry's *Hear Us O Lord*, may be another source of the device; at random, I find in *The Ambassadors* the phrases "a high distinguished polished impertinent reprobate" and "an isolated interesting attaching creature".

12 "The Light that Failed Not", *Leys Fortnightly*, 13 March 1925, p. 167.

13 Letter to Cape: *Selected Letters*, p. 85.

14 See Stephen Ullmann, *Language and Style* (Oxford, 1964), p. 196.

15 *The World and the Book* (London, 1971), p. 79.

16 Note by Lowry in MS. of incomplete novel "La Mordida".

17 Note in MS. of incomplete novel "The Ordeal of Sigbjørn Wilderness".

18 Fort, *The Book of the Damned* (New York, 1919), Chapter 1.

19 See William H. New, "Lowry, the Cabbala and Charles Jones", *Canadian Literature*, No. 43 (Winter 1970), pp. 83–7.

20 *Dark as the Grave* (London, 1969), pp. 154, 156.

21 An edited version of this story has been published in *Malcolm Lowry: Psalms and Songs* (New York, 1975).

22 There is a wild confusion in Douglas Day's *Malcolm Lowry: a Biography* (London, 1974), p. 117, where Grieg's translator is said to be "none other than A. G. Chater, Master of St. Catharine's" (where Lowry was an undergraduate from 1929 to 1932). Grieg's translator, A. G. Chater, had no relation to H. J. Chaytor, Senior Tutor of St. Catharine's in Lowry's time and later Master of the College.

An odd sidelight is that while at Cambridge Lowry published a poem, consisting largely of phrases appropriated from Grieg's novel, which earned the distinction of being damned by F. R. Leavis as "a curious mixture of Whitman and D. H. Lawrence . . . in the kind of free verse that is hardly verse" (*Cambridge Review*, 16 May 1930).

23 "Fiction Today", in *The Arts Today*, ed. Geoffrey Grigson (London, 1935), p. 115.

24 *Enemies of Promise* (London, 1938), p. 106.

25 *Selected Letters*, p. 28.

26 *Selected Letters*, p. 116; *Malcolm Lowry: The Man and His Work*, p. 112.

27   *Ushant: an essay* (New York, 1971), p. 350.
28   Aiken, *Collected Criticism* (London, 1968), pp. 202–3. The essay was first printed as "William Faulkner: the novel as form", *Atlantic*, 164 (November 1939), pp. 650–4.
29   *Ibid.*, p. 52.
30   *Selected Letters*, p. 173.

4

Malcolm Lowry and the Expressionist Vision

by SHERRILL E. GRACE

In 1969 George Woodcock entitled a study of Malcolm Lowry, "Art as the Writer's Mirror: Literary Solipsism in *Dark as the Grave*."[1] By singling out Lowry's solipsism, Woodcock focused upon an aspect of Lowry's art, more particularly his method, that many Lowry critics have noted. At the same time as he can legitimately be called a solipsist, Lowry can, and has been, described as a visionary. At first glance these terms—solipsist and visionary—seem contradictory. Furthermore, they can support opposing responses to his art: if we like him he is a visionary, if we do not he is a solipsist. But these two views of Lowry can be combined to enrich our understanding of his art. What is needed is a fresh critical approach. Lowry did not give us realist fiction either in *Volcano*, or in his other work. To call his work symbolist invites further problems for, as I shall show, Lowry uses image and symbol in a proliferating and autonomous way. Hallucination, dipsomania, and autobiography, with vision and prophecy, are also elements of his work. What I would like to suggest is that Lowry deliberately uses Expressionist techniques and embodies a strongly Expressionist vision in his work. To the extent that we can see him as an Expressionist, we can reconcile the visionary with the solipsist.

Undoubtedly, the most important criterion for discussing Lowry's Expressionism is that it enrich our understanding of his work. This must always be the primary aim, as well as a pleasure. An understanding of Lowry's Expressionism helps the critic to place Lowry within the broader context of Modernism. An analysis of Expressionism is also a study in the history of ideas, for Expressionism is an essential part of what is gathered under the umbrella term of Modernism. With these two goals in mind I have discussed the Expressionist context for Lowry's work. Secondly, I have compared the salient characteristics of Expressionism with his work, particularly *Under the Volcano*. Thirdly, I have discussed his writing more generally in terms of Expressionist film, by far the most important source of influence for Lowry's Expressionism. Finally, I have drawn some conclusions from these investigations which shed new light on Lowry.

What is Expressionism and how did Malcolm Lowry come under its influence? In his useful study *Expressionism*, John Willett distinguishes three uses of the word: a "family characteristic" of twentieth-century German art, a German movement lasting approximately from 1910–22, and a universal "quality of expressive emphasis and distortion".[2] For Lowry, it is the last two that are relevant with the second providing a special impetus for the third. In other words, Lowry wished to achieve a degree of "expressive emphasis and distortion" in *Volcano*, and elsewhere. Living when he did, he had an "arsenal of forms" at hand in the German Expressionist Movement. When Germanists speak of Expressionism they are concerned with the precursors: Strindberg whose dream plays were immensely popular; Edvard Munch, called by contemporaries "the father of Expressionism"; Baudelaire and Rimbaud (in particular *Bâteau Ivre*), and Dostoevsky who was widely translated in Germany and something of a rage by 1914. The chief exponents of Expressionism were in music Schoenberg and Berg (*Wozzeck* is a classic), in the fine arts Kandinsky, Ernst Ludwig Kirchner, Egon Schiele, Ludwig Meidner, Ernst Barlach, Oskar Kokoschka, in theatre and literature Kaiser, Toller, Hasenclever, the poets Heym and Trakl, and Heinrich Mann, Kafka and Döblin.[3] As regards cinema, there were a number of films, directors (Lang, Murnau, Weine), and actors (Werner Krauss, Paul Wegener, Conrad Veidt), whose names have become synonymous with cinematic Expressionism. According to Béla Balázs, the film is the true home of Expressionism, and in his *Das Kinobuch* of 1914, Kurt Pinthus emphasized the connexion between the success of the silent film and Expressionism.[4]

Generally speaking Expressionism conveys a radical sense of

unease on the part of the artist who feels that the world is terrifyingly inadequate. Whether his revolt against established systems takes an abstract or more doctrinaire form or resides in the passionate expression of inner protest and self-assertion, the artist conveys a new vision, usually shocking and disturbing, of reality. All Expressionists believed that human isolation and despair were threatening forces that must be faced honestly if ever man was to build a better world. Intellectually and artistically, Expressionism did not begin and end within Germany. As Wilhelm Worringer argued in *Abstraktion und Einfühlung* (written in 1906), the urge to abstraction (a principle of Expressionism) surfaces periodically in human history, for example in Gothic art and architecture. Expressionism and Romanticism are in many ways close cousins while Surrealism, another branch of Modernism, has striking stylistic affinities with Expressionism.[5] The roots of Expressionism are wide and deep. It flowered briefly in England as Vorticism, as well as in the early plays of Eugene O'Neill and the paintings of the Mexican, Oroxco. It is no accident that Expressionism arose concurrently with Marinetti's Futurism, the researches of Freud and Jung, the phenomenology of Husserl, and under the strong influence of Kant and Nietzsche.

Although one could argue on stylistic terms alone that *Volcano*, and some of Lowry's other writings, are expressionistic, there are extra-textual reasons for doing so. Lowry had some knowledge of and considerable interest in Expressionist painting, theatre, music, and film. He knew the work of Munch, Schoenberg, Berg, the writing of Rimbaud, Strindberg, Dostoevsky, Wedekind (another precursor), and the plays of Toller, Kaiser and O'Neill whose *The Hairy Ape* and *Emperor Jones* were special favourites. He discovered O'Neill during his teens and in 1925 he saw the London production of Kaiser's *From Morn till Midnight* starring Claude Rains. This expressionistic production would provide an interesting motif for *October Ferry*. During his stay in Bonn in 1928, he became familiar with German Expressionist theatre and film, and was deeply impressed by a Köln production of O'Neill's *The Great God Brown*.[6] His interest in a group of writers less known for their links with Expressionism is more remarkable—Maeterlinck and Hermann Bang (a surprising link), Oscar Wilde, Oswald Spengler, and Poe are all considered to be forerunners of the movement.[7] The most important influence, however, was the wonderful-horrible

German Expressionist film: *The Cabinet of Dr. Caligari* (1919), *From Morn till Midnight* (1920, based upon Kaiser's play), *Waxworks* (1921), *Nosferatu* (1922), *Warning Shadows* (1922), *The Street* (1923), *The Hands of Orlac* (1924), *The Student of Prague* (1926). These, among others, provided Lowry with a cornucopia of effects, themes, and allusions.

In order to discuss the influence of Expressionism, a method must be evolved that will be as simple and clear as possible. Ulrich Weisstein prefers to emphasize the analysis of style whereas Walter Sokel emphasizes thematic analysis. It is possible to have it both ways. No analysis of this fascinating movement is complete without reference to themes as well as aesthetics. Critics agree that Expressionism, in theory and practice, marks a sharp break with previous styles: Expressionism is non-mimetic and therefore in revolt against Realism, Naturalism, and Impressionism. In Herbert Read's words, the Expressionist artist does not wish to reproduce "the objective reality of the world, but the subjective reality of the feelings which objects and events arouse. . . ."[8] In the following discussion, distinctions can be maintained between aesthetics and epistemology, stylistic devices and techniques, and theme. The influence of Expressionism upon Lowry is apparent in all three areas.

"In order to qualify as a bona fide Expressionist," according to Ulrich Weisstein,

> an artist must reject the mimetic approach. Thus epistemologically, E. undermines the foundations of realistic art. . . . What Expressionist art seeks to render visible, however, are soul states and the violent emotions welling up from the innermost recesses of the subconscious. . . .[9]

Following Kant reality for the Expressionist resides primarily in the mind of the perceiver, not in the observable, objective world, nor in universals. Although the existence of an objective world is not denied and may, in fact, be used by the artist, it is present only insofar as it evokes an inner reality. In 1917 Kasimir Edschmid distinguished Expressionism from Naturalism thus: *"So wird der Raum des expressionistischen Künstlers Vision. Er sieht nicht wieder, er schaut. Er schildert nicht, er erlebt. Er gibt nicht wieder,*

*er gestaltet. Er nimmt nicht, er sucht. Nun gibt es nicht mehr die
Kette der Tatsachen. . . . Nun gibt es die Vision davon.*"[10] Thus,
the art form projects the tensions between inner and outer realities.
The artist strives to break down the boundaries between a subjective and objective reality and to superimpose subjective reality
upon the external world. Where realist art inevitably tries to
efface its artifice, Expressionist art draws attention to itself as art.

Lowry's aesthetic position and his formal endeavours parallel
this basic Expressionist position. He makes it clear in his letters
that he is "in rebellion" against the realist novel: "unquestionably
what one is after is a new form, a new approach to reality itself."[11]
In Lowry's view, reality was dynamic and perpetually protean.
Furthermore, although he ignored neither an external objective
reality nor a possible spiritual realm of universals, his method for
understanding, accommodating, or articulating these areas was
solipsistic. He began with the perceptions of the autobiographical
self and inner vision. The chief protagonist of his projected masterwork *The Voyage That Never Ends* was to embody the unconscious
human urge to constant creation of a self that would reflect the
dynamic essence of life.[12]

Following on from basic epistemological similarities, there are
many stylistic and thematic parallels between Lowry's work and
Expressionism. One of the most interesting of these is the handling of character. In his "apologia" on *Under the Volcano*, Lowry
went to considerable lengths to clarify his use of character: "The
truth is that the character drawing is not only weak but virtually nonexistent . . . the four main characters being intended, in
one of the book's meanings, to be aspects of the same man" (p. 60).
He goes on to explain that the characters represent the unconscious and that the novel is concerned "with the forces in man
which cause him to be terrified of himself".

The Expressionist artist is totally disinterested in the psychological, and therefore realistic, development of the individual character. Similarly, Lowry was not interested in offering an etiology
for his heroes who are three-dimensional only insofar as re-
quired for the "superficial plane" of his work. Apparently Lowry
felt that fiction could not entirely reject a certain recognizable
reality without losing its readers, and this view seems to have
been shared by many Expressionist dramatists and most prose
writers. Of foremost interest to the Expressionist is the portrayal

of individual soul states which also embody collective or cosmic forces. Jan Joseph Lipski has described this paradox clearly:

> Hence it is characteristic for E. to depict reality as reduced to the "I". But the "I", which is the subject of Expressionist literature, tends to identify itself with communal values and values of a cosmic nature, with the universal soul acting as a cosmic force, etc. Thus the dialectics of extreme subjectivism pitted against universal tendencies is essential for the movement.[13]

Here again, Lowry's intention is comparable. Geoffrey Firmin embodies and represents the soul of modern Western man on the brink of the abyss. As his familiars remind us, Geoffrey is Faustian and we are watching the battle of good and evil within his dying soul.

Before moving on from this Expressionist concern with self (or an "I" who is both self and cosmic force), it is interesting to note the Expressionist predilection for self-portraiture and split-selves (*doppelgängers*). Weisstein suggests that self-portraiture is important to the Expressionist because, "it is precisely the soul . . . especially the soul in writhing anguish" that he wishes to project.[14] The literary vehicle for this concern with self is autobiography and few writers have been as intensely autobiographical as Lowry. The device of the split-self in portraiture, or the *doppelgänger* in literature, is a way of projecting the image of the "I" as both self and other (e.g. cosmic or Faustian force). Wilde's *Dorian Gray*, O'Neill's *The Great God Brown*, and Weine's film *The Student of Prague* offer "characters" who can watch their inner destruction unfold in a *doppelgänger*. Lowry's use of the *doppelgänger* device is more general and metaphorical. Although Hugh is Geoffrey's *doppelgänger*, Geoffrey's tendency is to perceive whatever is external to the self as a fragment or reflection of the self. In his agony, he sees himself,

> surrounded in delirium by these phantoms of himself, the policemen, Fructuoso Sanabria, that other man who looked like a poet, the luminous skeleton, even the rabbit in the corner and the ash and sputum on the filthy floor—did not each correspond, in a way he couldn't understand yet obscurely recognized, to some fraction of his being?[15]

Here the emphasis falls upon the isolation and terrible alienation of the split-self.

There are a number of stylistic elements common to Expressionist painting, literature and film, that Lowry used to great effect. The first is deliberate disruption of spatial and temporal continuities. The spatial disruption is obvious in the grotesque distortions which are such a striking feature of all Expressionist art. Inner and outer, real and fantastic, become confused and inter-changed in the effort to superimpose subjective reality upon the objective world. As the human figure becomes less real, sets and landscapes become increasingly expressive—symbolic diagrams of emotional states. For example, in the paintings of Barlach of Schmidt-Rottluff, or in O'Neill's *Emperor Jones*, landscapes appear to be alive and menacing. In *Under the Volcano* the entire landscape mirrors Geoffrey's confusion as well as seeming to participate in his destruction. Popocatapetl becomes Moby Dick; a sunflower stares at Geoffrey "like God"; his surroundings taunt:

> Why am I here, says the silence, what have I done echoes the emptiness, why have I ruined myself in this wilful manner, chuckles the money in the till, why have I been brought so low, wheedles the thoroughfare. . . .
>
> (p. 359)

Part of Geoffrey's problem is his projection of inner confusion upon external reality.

The disruption of temporal continuities is even more important. For the Expressionist, time and historical process are dynamic: "history past and present is regarded as a continual struggle between good and evil" while "time and its dynamic unfolding [are] constitutive agents in the struggle of good with evil. . . ."[16] Therefore, Expressionists will depict contradictions through dynamic forms and technique. Lowry also believed that reality was dynamic and that time must flow for life and art to continue.[17] Kaiser's *Von Morgens bis Mitternachts* is an excellent example of temporal discontinuity for there are no bridges or explanations between the "stations" or scenes of the play. Kafka's *The Trial* creates a similar effect. In *Under the Volcano*, Lowry went to considerable lengths to break up the reader's sense of temporal continuity by constructing twelve self-enclosed chapters. The impression of stasis that results from this temporal discontinuity mirrors the *acedia* of Geoffrey's soul. Similarly, the effect in Kaiser's play, as in so much Expressionist art is, paradoxically, that of stasis. In Lowry's case, the stasis has an important thematic purpose: Geoff, like the world, has "bogged down" forgetting Goethe's words, *"Wer immer strebend sich bemüht, den können wir erlösen."*

There are many stylistic devices common to Expressionism— telegraph style, framing devices, mirrors, clocks and staircases, whirling fairgrounds—that, along with double focus and visual effects, are especially obvious in Expressionist films. Some of these are examined below. The characteristic telegraph style of jerky, abrupt exclamation is most successful in poetry or drama and less common in prose. A German example is Hans Fallada's *Der junge Goedeschal* (1920):

> He staggered. Garishly lit houses loomed up out of the dark as if seen from a speeding train. . . . No resting place! Stumbling, falling forward, he began to run, brushed past walls whose pores seemed to exude a sweaty slime.[18]

Similar examples of a telegraph style are found in Lowry. The most extensive use of this stylistic device is in *Ultramarine*, especially in Chapter III, where it contributes to our sense of Dana's disturbed, whirling perceptions. Even in *Under the Volcano* where the dominant style is that of long, circling, convoluted sentences, clause piled on clause, Lowry uses brief telegraphic passages to suggest the confusion of Geoffrey's mind (for example, the fair scene in VII and the toilet scene in X). The most striking example of the telegraph style, however, comes in an early work, the story "June the 30th, 1934." Bill Goodyear returning to England by boat and train is pursued and disturbed by reports of Hitler's atrocities and the imminence of war, by his travelling companion Firmin, and by visions of his son. He feels himself undergoing a strange transformation. The final passages of the story dramatize the fusion of his disturbed mind with the rhythm of the train as it screams "like a shell, through a metal world":

> His eyes returned to the window. A man digging, sharply illumined by a shower of sparks like red blossoms, slowly raised his spade. . . . It's never too late, never too late. To start again. You bore in the earth. Silver and copper. Silver and gold. Man makes his cross. With crucible steel. Base metal; counterfeit; manganese; chromium; makes his iron cross; with crucible steel.
>
> The train took a hill. The boy fell in the fire. The knitting needles flashed like bayonets. Steel wool. The red lights flashed. Green lights. Knit. Socks! Knit. Shroud! Knit. Stab! Iron, steel,

said the train. Iron, steel. Iron, tin, iron, tin. Steel and iron steel and iron steel and iron steel and iron steeeeeeeel! . . .[19]

In his study *Expressionism*, R. S. Furness describes the concept of image as *"expressive* rather than imitative, existing as a powerful, autonomous figure of speech from which radiate a host of evocative meanings".[20] The metaphor, or image, rather than functioning as a mirror of objective reality with a specific referent, becomes independent. Through proliferating associations a world of subjective meaning emerges. The expressive image is precisely what we find in Lowry. These autonomous images with constantly expanding associations make *Under the Volcano* a challenge to some and a frustration to others who prefer to tie down symbols. Lowry explained some of the associations of his wheels, of the number twelve, of the entire novel in his letter to Cape. The image of the volcano is a rich example—it is Popocatapetl with ancient Mexican associations, it is Mount Aetna with Tartarus at its base, it is Moby Dick a great white whale pursuing and beckoning Geoffrey, it is the Mountain of Delight for Geoffrey the pilgrim, it is a type of Mecca (the small Mexican town of Amecameca is at its base), it is "the mighty mountain Himavat" that Geoffrey believes he is climbing as he dies. This volcano is, at once, the perfect image of Geoffrey's mind and soul and of "the world itself . . . bursting, bursting into black spouts of villages catapulted into space" (p. 375). Fully in keeping with an Expressionist aesthetic, this autonomous image embodies the dialectics of the "I" and the universal forces of destruction loose in a pre-World War II world. The volcano image may only be understood centripetally, as it is developed within the novel, and always with attention to its expanding nature.

Before turning to an examination of Lowry and Expressionist film, let us look briefly at the themes of Expressionism. Here the parallels with Lowry's fiction are so obvious as to need little comment. The world of Expressionism is one of madness and degeneration. Mad Doctors, megalomaniacs and murderers abound. Despite a recurrent emphasis on apocalypse, the *"Aufbruch"* of the Expressionist, this awakening, more often than not is without positive result. Much stronger is the love of death especially self-destruction, in and for itself. The apocalyptic, but ironic, ending of *Volcano*, with Geoffrey's scream recalling Munch, is a case in point. Equally important is the theme of impotence. The heroes suffer from sexual impotence and/or a sexuality that is tortured and masochistic. Moreover, this impotence marks a general failure of love and of the spirit: *"No se puede vivir sin amar."* As Walter Sokel suggests, spiritual and emotional impotence involves the hero in a desperate longing to become his opposite, the direct man of action who is capable of love.[21] This same impotence also results in violent male/female struggles with variations upon themes of adultery, castration and vampirism. The characters embody universal warring male and female forces with the female invariably threatening to overwhelm the male (for example, Strindberg, Munch, Kokoschka, early Kaiser). Father/son conflicts frequently arise (for example, Hasenclever's *Der Sohn,* Kaiser's *Gas*). Cityscapes, as well as landscapes, are presented non-mimetically as deathscapes. In general, the dynamic energy of Expressionism leads to themes of tension, conflict, violent awakenings of the soul coupled with a splitting of the self, and above all wilful self-destruction. This is essentially the world that one finds in *Ultramarine, Lunar Caustic,* and *Under the Volcano.*

There are at least three distinct types of film influence apparent in Lowry's work—thematic, stylistic, and epistemological. The first arises from the numerous allusions to particular Expressionist films such as *Caligari, From Morn till Midnight, The Student of Prague, The Street, The Hands of Orlac, Sunrise, Warning Shadows, Metropolis.* There are a few notable exceptions—Griffith, and Epstein's *The Fall of the House of Usher,* to mention only two—but references to the German film dominate. When viewing these film classics one is struck by the recurrence of settings, themes, and specific forms of conflict. Murder and suicide occur regularly. The murderers and suicides are invariably haunted, obsessed, and guilty souls tormented by their overweening desires and persecuted by forces around them. In his *Classics of the Horror Film,* William Everson describes *Caligari* and *The Hands of Orlac* as "Mad-Doctor" films. Troubled marriages or doomed love affairs are another popular subject, from Murnau's *Sunrise,* Robison's *Warning Shadows,* and Grüne's *The Street* to, once again, *Caligari* and *Orlac.* Often the jealous husband or lover has a rival and is about to be betrayed. Other ingredients of these films are *doppelgängers,* mirrors and threatening shadows, framing devices for the main story, circus scenes with whirling ferris wheels, constant hallucination and delirium for the protagonist, and distorted landscapes achieved with stylized studio sets and special lighting effects.

There are obvious parallels between the themes and settings in these films and the themes and certain scenes in Lowry's fiction. Often the allusion is made clear as when Geoffrey likens Laruelle's house to something from *The Cabinet of Dr. Caligari*. More often the allusion is oblique, only fully appreciated if one is lucky enough to have seen the film. In *October Ferry* where he alludes to many films, Lowry may have been thinking of German Expressionist film when Ethan sees his face in the rear view mirror as "Its lips silently formed the one word: 'Murderer!'" (*October Ferry*, 216). In Fritz Lang's *M* (1931), *Caligari*, and *The Street*, the word "murderer" appears suddenly and ominously on signs in the centre of the screen, or as a subtitle.

The stylistic influence of film upon Lowry's work brings two distinct aspects of his narrative to mind. There is first that visual, typographical quality that Stephen Spender noticed. Lowry used signs, advertisements etc. in a way recalling the captions and subtitles of silent films. The visual quality is obvious in *Under the Volcano* and has been discussed by Lowry critics. It is even more apparent in *October Ferry to Gabriola*. The results of Lowry's "spatial effects", making narrative material visually distinct and emphatic on the space of the page, are varied and interesting. It should also be noted that Expressionist art is generally a highly visual art.

Second, in the German Expressionist films sets, lighting, acting, and camera work were used to create a private universe for, as Lotte Eisner explains in *The Haunted Screen*, Expressionism "does not adapt itself to a world already in existence". In Lowry's fiction the "world" is usually a projection of the individual perceptions of his characters. At the same time, the fairground scene in Chapter VII of *Volcano*, like the fairground in *Caligari* and in several of these films, symbolizes not only a madly revolving world perceived by the protagonist, but the helplessness of the individual soul caught up in superior whirling forces. Lowry's famous solipsism, seen from the point of view of Expressionism and the German films, is closely allied to the dialectics of subjective and universal tendencies essential to an Expressionist style.

In some of his earlier work Lowry does refer to films but in *Lunar Caustic*, he handles the thematic and stylistic influence of film in ways both more sophisticated and more integral to this purpose.[22] The novella falls into three distinct sections. The first and last portray Plantagenet before and after the hospital experience with the last section repeating several details (e.g. the bar, the old lady, the church) from the first. Together they frame the central action, setting off and emphasizing the world of the insane. This framing technique casts an ironic note over the entire story, for Plantagenet gains nothing from his pilgrimage and the world outside appears as threatening as the hospital. Within the hospital section five separate scenes are presented from Plantagenet's uncertain point of view. First impressions of the ward, disturbed by hallucination and fantasy, gradually give way to the puppet show, followed by the episode at the piano and the discussion with Claggart. The fifth scene occurs at the hospital window, as Plantagenet watches the storm. There may be several influences at work in Lowry's description of the puppet show, but one of particular interest is Robison's film *Warning Shadows*, which introduces the characters as shadows on a stage. Huge shadow hands take the characters away. The sense of mysterious control is ominous. Several times Plantagenet is disturbed by a giant hand snatching the puppets from the stage during the show.

The central metaphor of *Lunar Caustic* is that of the madhouse. Depending upon one's perception, the entire world can seem more mad than an asylum. Certainly, a madhouse is the perfect expression of a confused consciousness and a distraught soul. Lowry's use of the hospital in *Lunar Caustic* bears a striking resemblance to *The Cabinet of Dr. Caligari*. In *Caligari*, the main story of the mad Doctor and his somnambulist is set off by a framing device. The movie opens with two men talking. One begins the strange account of his life and then the scene fades to a fairground and the story of Caligari. At the end, we return to these men who turn out to be inmates of an asylum. The Director of the hospital, now in white coat, looks exactly like the madman Caligari. Is the story merely the result of a diseased mind, or an acute portrayal of the real nature of authority? Is the world really a place of such horror or is this madness the reflection of an obsessed soul? The distinction between madness and sanity, subjective and objective reality, is disturbingly blurred. It is no coincidence that in the context of *Lunar Caustic* Plantagenet says to Claggart: "There are always two sides, *nicht wahr, Herr Doktor*, to a show like this?"[23]

Among the films of obvious importance to *Under the Volcano* are *Caligari*, *The Hands of Orlac* (with *Mad Love*, 1935, the Hollywood remake starring Peter Lorre, central to *Volcano*) and *Sunrise*. Their influence on the *Volcano* is both thematic and stylistic. Each of these films portrays the essentially Expressionist subject of a catacylsmic struggle within man's soul or mind. The stories are invariably macabre—a mad mountebank-doctor unleashes a murderous somnambulist, a musician with the grafted hands of a murderer goes mad. The characters operate less as individuals, despite the projection of subjective states of dream, hallucination, and madness, than as symbols of universal problems, social ills, or disturbed psychic states. The acting is exaggerated and stylized. The settings are often non-realistic studio sets of geometric shapes. Mirrors, whirling fairgrounds, double and multiple exposures and chiaroscuro create the sensation of a landscape alive with menacing power; the landscape mirrors the turmoil of the soul at the same time as it *appears* to embody evil and hostile forces.

Mad Love is both the "hieroglyphic of the times" in its portrayal of power and obsession, and a thematic parallel for the story of Geoffrey and Yvonne. Apart from Peter Lorre's magnificent portrayal of Doctor Gogol it is a weak film, but Lowry had also seen the original *Hands of Orlac* starring Conrad Veidt. The story involves a mad Doctor Gogol who grafts a murderer's hands onto an injured pianist Stephen Orlac. Under this terrible influence, Orlac kills his father. Gogol meanwhile is determined to possess Orlac's beautiful actress wife, Yvonne. After her repeated refusals to betray her husband, the Doctor attempts to destroy the artist, and then tries to strangle Yvonne while the refrain "Each man kills the thing he loves" echoes in his mind. Gogol does not succeed with his evil intentions because Orlac arrives just in time to save his wife. *Under the Volcano* offers no such facile conclusion. Destruction and betrayal, once set in motion, grind out a tragic conclusion; Geoffrey *does* kill the thing he loves.

In 1928 Lowry saw Fred Murnau's *Sonnenaufgang* which he said had influenced him "almost as much as any book [he] ever read".[24] In Chapter XI of the 1940 version of *Volcano* there are several references to *Sunrise*. Although the overt references were cut,

THE ART OF MALCOLM LOWRY

Chapter XI of the final version opens with the cryptic direction
"SUNSET" and in Chapter VII, as the Consul views El Farolito in
his mind's eye, he remembers a sunrise he had watched from there,
"a slow bomb bursting over the Sierra Madre—*Sonnenaufgang!*"
(p. 214). Although Murnau's *Sunrise* was not the only film to make
its way into the *Volcano* (Laruelle's house looks like something from
The Cabinet of Dr. Caligari, and *Las Manos de Orlac* is omni-
present), it is probably a more profound influence. Murnau's subject is an adulterous marriage in which "The Man"—none of the
characters has a name thereby universalizing the theme—attempts
to kill his unwanted "Wife." Double exposures produce the effect
of good and evil battling for possession of the man's soul. The man's
tortured form takes on symbolic proportions and the landscape
comes to life via menacing lighting effects. The couple are reconciled after near disaster and, while they gaze at wedding photographs in a window, there is a sequence which resembles Lowry's
handling of double exposure in the Chapter II scene with Yvonne.
As she and Geoffrey pause outside the printer's shop, Yvonne per-
ceives their reflected image:

> They stood, as once, looking in. . . . From the mirror within the
> window an ocean creature so drenched and coppered by sun and
> winnowed by sea-wind and spray looked back at her she seemed,
> even while making the fugitive motions of Yvonne's vanity, some-
> where beyond human grief charioting the surf. But the sun turned
> grief to poison and a glowing body only mocked the sick heart,
> Yvonne knew, if the sun-darkened creature of waves and sea
> margins and windows did not! In the window itself, on either
> side of this abstracted gaze of her mirrored face, the same brave
> wedding invitations she remembered were ranged . . . but this
> time there was something she hadn't seen before, which the
> Consul now pointed out with a murmur of "Strange'. . . .
>
> (p. 61)

The image of Yvonne in the present moment and in the near
and more distant past is superimposed upon the photographs and
invitations within the window. These, in turn, are seen against
the enlargement of *"La Despedida"*—"set behind and above the
already spinning flywheel of the presses . . ." (p. 61). Reflected
in the window, Yvonne sees Geoffrey and herself as they once
were: "They stood, as once, looking in." She sees herself as she

has recently been, "coppered by sun and winnowed by sea-wind". There is even the suggestion that a completely different Yvonne appears in the window, a Venus-like Yvonne "somewhere beyond human grief charioting the surf". But moving forward through these fragmented images of Yvonne's personality, these other selves, are further levels of present and past reality—the photographs and invitations linking past to present, the spinning flywheel which temporally precedes the invitations, the ancient glacial rock, at one time whole, now split by fire. Through this double exposure technique Lowry portrays the Expressionist dialectic of subjectivism and cosmic force. *"La Despedida"* is an excellent image of the forces overwhelming the world; the superimposition of the image of the split rock on the reflection of Yvonne and Geoffrey implies that it is an equally apt image of the internal forces destroying these two people.

The third influence of film on Lowry's art is epistemological in two senses. The first and most important is what I call the dramatizing of epistemological problems, but Lowry seems to have had an additional factor in mind. In *October Ferry* (p. 61), Ethan speaks of films as having more reality than life and of novels as having no reality at all. In his letters, Lowry speaks of a new approach to reality, and in his 1951 *Work in Progress* statement, he speaks of his novels as films. *Volcano* can be seen as a film of Geoffrey's life, and the *Voyage* as the film of Sigbjørn Wilderness' life. Lowry felt that films somehow captured reality better than novels, probably for the simple reason that they move and therefore present, better than other art forms, the illusion of dynamic, ever-changing reality.

A discussion of Expressionist film focuses upon the central question of epistemological problems. This influence of the film brings one back to the non-mimetic foundation of Expressionism, and to Lowry's art. The epistemological question is especially significant for film because it is the nature of the medium to comment upon these problems. Early film-makers were well aware of the film's capacity to reproduce objective reality, as well as to produce an alternate or independent reality. They often exploited the tension between the two in order to explore the nature of the self and the ways in which we perceive. *The Cabinet of Dr. Caligari* is a classic example. The asylum frame forces the viewer to question the "reality" of what he has seen. Thus, the film creates a commentary between text and subtext, a dramatizing of epistemological problems.

The dramatizing of epistemological problems, apparent throughout Lowry's work, is most comparable to film in *Under the Volcano*. Here we witness the movie of Geoffrey's life, not simply in terms of externals and certainly not with a precise etiology, but as the expression of his soul which becomes synonymous with Western man on the brink of the abyss. A highly charged dialectic is maintained between text and subtext, between outer and inner reality. The toilet scene in Chapter X is a splendid example. Although one can scarcely speak of this scene as framed by the rest of the chapter—the scene is quite short—it is set off on either side by the objective reality of the Salón Ofélia and the meal with Yvonne and Hugh. Disruption of temporal and spatial continuities together with a jerky telegraph style create the sense of extreme distortion and confusion in the Consul's mescal fogged mind. By this point in the novel, however, it is clear that Lowry is telling us "something new about hellfire" as well as about dipsomania. This scene is far more than a mimetic rendering of a drunken mind. Geoffrey is Christ, Faust, Prometheus, Western man. The superimposition of inner reality upon the outer reality of tourist folder, railway schedule, indeed of the entire day, expresses his agony and forces the reader to perceive his personal horror *and* the universal implications of his vision. To what extent is there truth in this madness? To what extent are we all locked within distorted perception? As with *Caligari* we are forced to question our own perceptions and the very nature of reality.

It is the mark of a truly great writer that no *single* source or influence should dominate his art. Expressionism is only one aspect of Lowry's fictional world together with the Cabbala, a stern Protestantism, and mescal. Expressionism may, however, be more important than these other factors. Certainly, Expressionism was a profound and lasting influence that shaped Lowry's vision and his technique. Even in as late a work as *October Ferry* we find a distraught Ethan questioning his perceptions; it seems "as if the subjective world within . . . [has] somehow turned itself inside out: as if the objective world without [has] itself caught a sort of hysteria" (p. 116). Ethan immediately thinks of *The Hairy Ape* and Claude Rains in *From Morn till Midnight.* Such explicit references confirm Lowry's continuing interest in Expressionism. Lowry also employs an Expressionist style in many scenes of *October Ferry* (e.g. in XVIII and XXXI) in order to portray the tumult within Ethan's soul. These scenes mark stages of distress in his struggle for spiritual and psychic rebirth.

The strong Expressionism in *Under the Volcano* can be seen in a similar light. To be sure, Lowry created a truly Expressionist hero in Geoffrey and provided, through his eyes, an Expressionist vision. But *Volcano* is also a stage in a much longer journey— *The Voyage That Never Ends.* Geoffrey's failure to progress can in part be attributed to his Expressionist vision and limitations. Unable to distinguish between self and not self, unable to act or to love, he wills his destruction. To this extent, Lowry used Expressionism deliberately and critically. The question remains whether Lowry himself managed to control and outgrow his enthusiasm for Expressionism. Expressionism was definitely a movement of the young, and most artists moved on to other styles and themes after a period of intense involvement. With Lowry the case is less clear. While *Hear Us O Lord* strives for a vision of harmony and *October Ferry* incorporates Expressionist scenes within a larger whole, Lowry was never able to finish these works. His greatest work is *Under the Volcano,* a distorted vision of collapse.

The Expressionist vision of madness and degeneration appealed profoundly to Lowry. Like Geoffrey, Lowry was finally incapable of achieving a new balance. At the same time, his Expressionism explains why Lowry is no detached formalist like so many modernists. He puts his own soul on the line, and in so doing, shares the deep Expressionist concern for humanity. Like the Expressionists he sought the religious in life, finding it not in organized religion, but in the worship of the human/cosmic soul. By understanding Lowry's affinity with Expressionism, we can better appreciate his special blend of solipsism and vision, autobiography and prophecy. This blend characterizes his method and his position as a modernist. Expressionism, then, is one of the elements necessary for an understanding of Lowry's art. It is also necessary for the eventual *"Gestalt"* reading of a twentieth-century masterpiece portraying, in Lowry's words, "the forces in man which cause him to be terrified of himself [. . . and] the ultimate fate of mankind".

NOTES

1 See *Malcolm Lowry: The Man and His Work*, ed. George Woodcock (1971).

2 John Willett, *Expressionism* (1970), p. 8.

3 The following works have been most useful for this study: Armin Arnold, *Prosa des Expressionismus* (1972); Béla Balázs, *Theory of the Film* (1972); Lotte Eisner, *The Haunted Screen* (1969); William K. Everson, *Classics of the Horror Film* (1974); R. S. Furness, *Expressionism* (1973); Siegfried Kracauer, *From Caligari to Hitler* (1947); Rudolf Kurtz, *Expressionismus und Film* (1965), orig. 1926; Roger Manvell and Heinrich Fraenkel, *The German Cinema* (1971); Victor H. Meisel, *Voices of German Expressionism* (1970); Kurt Pinthus, *Das Kinobuch* (1963), orig. 1914; Paul Raabe, ed., *The Era of Expressionism* (1974); Walter H. Sokel, *The Writer in Extremis* (1959); Mardi Valgemae, *Accelerated Grimace: Expressionism in the American Drama of the 1920's* (1972); John Willett, *Expressionism* (1970), Ulrich Weisstein, ed., *Expressionism as an International Literary Phenomenon* (1973). I would also like to thank McGill University for a travel grant enabling me to attend the 1977 Houston German Expressionism Symposium.

4 See Béla Balázs *Der unsichtbare Mensch oder die Kultur des Films* (Vienna and Leipsig, 1924, p. 88—"*das einzige Gebiet, vielleicht die einzig recht-mässige Heimat des Expressionismus.*" I am grateful to Professor Charles Helmetag and his paper, "Walter Hasenclever, an Expressionist Filmwriter" presented at the 1977 Houston Expressionism Symposium, for this information.

5 Both Surrealism and Dadism should be distinguished methodologically from Expressionism which embraced a volitional view of the artist in sharp distinction to the automatism of the Surrealists and a dynamic historical process as opposed to the Dadaist world of chance. These distinctions are discussed further in a work-in-progress on Expressionism and its North American influence.

6 See Lowry's remarks in his 1951 letter to Clenens ten Holder, *Selected Letters of Malcolm Lowry*, eds. Harvey Breit and Margerie Bonner Lowry (1965), pp. 238–9. For a discussion of the London Kaiser production with Rains, see R. S. Furness, *Expressionism*, p. 86. In his essay, "Expressionism in English Drama and Prose Literature", Breon Mitchell points out that "German Expressionist drama formed a major part of the theatrical life of London in the twenties", *Expressionism as an International Literary Phenomenon*, p. 183.

7 For the influence of Maeterlinck see Armin Arnold *Prosa des Expressionismus*, p. 46. In his essay, "Foreign Influences on German Expressionist Prose", *Expressionism as an International Literary Phenomenon*, pp. 84–5, Professor Arnold points out that Bang's novels and Jack London's supermen were popular with Expressionists.

8 *The Philosophy of Modern Art* (1963), p. 51. Lowry was aware of Read's theories.

9   *Expressionism as an International Literary Phenomenon*, p. 23.

10 Quoted in Furness, *Expressionism*, p. 23. *"Er nimmt nicht, er sucht"*—
    the Expressionist does not merely accept or receive what he perceives,
    but actively seeks the essences of things.

11 *Selected Letters*, p. 68 and p. 330. In *October Ferry to Gabriola* (1970),
    p. 61, Ethan insists that, "A novelist presents less of life the more
    closely he approaches what he thinks of as his realism."

12 For a more detailed discussion of Lowry's aesthetics, see my article
    "The Creative Process: An Introduction to Time and Space in Malcolm
    Lowry's Fiction", *Studies in Canadian Literature* (Winter, 1977), pp.
    61–8. Lowry was influenced, through Conrad Aiken, by Bergson who
    had considerable influence upon Expressionism and Vorticism.

13 "Expressionism in Poland", *Expressionism as an International Literary
    Phenomenon*, p. 301. Lipski offers many valuable insights into the nature
    of Expressionism and distinguishes it from symbolism in terms of its
    dualism, dynamism, and reverence for time.

14 *Expressionism as an International Literary Phenomenon*, p. 41.

15 *Under the Volcano* (1963), p. 362. Subsequent references are in the text.

16 Lipski, *Expressionism as an International Literary Phenomenon*, p. 301.

17 I examine the importance of time in "The Creative Process" (see 10),
    and in *"Under the Volcano:* Narrative Mode and Technique", *Journal
    of Canadian Fiction* (Spring, 1973), 57–61.

18 Quoted and translated in Willett, *Expressionism*, p. 150. Arnold offers
    further examples in *Prosa des Expressionismus*.

19 "June the 30th, 1934", *Psalms and Songs*, ed. Margerie Lowry (1975),
    p. 48.

20 *Expressionism*, p. 18.

21 Sokel, *The Writer in Extremis*, p. 121.

22 References to film occur in *Ultramarine* and the early stories. In 1949–
    50 Lowry prepared a filmscript of *Tender is the Night*. The TS and
    Notes contain references to Expressionist films and Lowry's treatment
    of the novel is expressionistic in style and purpose.

23 *Lunar Caustic* (1963), p. 47.

24 *Selected Letters*, p. 239.

5

The Own Place of the Mind: An Essay in Lowrian Topography

by GEORGE WOODCOCK

Thinking of Malcolm Lowry, one is often tempted by the familiar Miltonic tag, "The mind is its own place, and in itself/Can make a heav'n of hell, a hell of heav'n." The mind "is its own *place*" not "its own *person*", for hell and heaven alike exist, in the grand Miltonic and Dantesque topographies, as realms where personality has reached its end. Lowry, as I shall suggest, is a writer for whom personality, the common concern of the novelists, becomes increasingly less important and less attainable in fictional terms outside the author's imprisoning self, but for whom place—not merely as a reflected state of mind—but also in its physically apprehensible sense becomes increasingly important.

At its most intense, the visual imagery of Lowry's fiction takes on such a super-real quality of inner illumination that it is easy for those not familiar with the actual Mexico of *Under the Volcano* or the actual fragment of Canada where "The Forest Path to the Spring" is set to believe that everything is the invention of a brilliantly fertile imagination, presenting a series of dream landscapes where nightmares can be enacted without relationship to the world of here and now. But when one knows the places, such an assumption is impossible. Like other great writers on Hell and Heaven, Lowry never fell into the error of dividing in man the physical from the spiritual, either in his apprehension of existence or in his presentation of it, and so he did not merely take convenient images from his Canadian setting to create the state of mind—the elegiac mood—of "the Forest Spring"; the actual experience of the setting as Lowry lived himself into it shaped the novella, and the cougar is a physical beast as well as an inner terror. In the case of Mexico,

112

I have already, in *Odysseus Ever Returning* (1970), examined the detailed way in which Lowry describes the actual environment so that it emerges not merely as a natural background but also as a present and active element in the tragedy of Geoffrey Firmin.

The inclination among critics to neglect the importance of the perceived environment, of place in its most direct and concrete sense, in Lowry's work has been encouraged by the accounts of some of his acquaintances who failed to understand his eccentric means of perception. James Stern, who wandered with him about Paris and New York, thought Lowry was totally lacking in a sense of place. "Unlike mine, his bump of locality on land was erratic." And his French translator, Clarisse Françillon, disappointed with Lowry's unenthusiastic response to her efforts to show him the sights of her beloved Paris, concluded that "He preferred his own inner landscape and orbit, sampling the cantinas", and "sun and trees, these he no longer knew how to appreciate—he never looked out of the window."

Clarisse Françillon's remarks—which no-one who had seen Lowry within the landscape of "The Forest Path" could have made —referred to a visit in Paris in 1948, when he had still a great deal of writing ahead of him which showed an almost hypersensitive responsiveness to the places where he lived with a degree of passion. Such assumptions of Lowry's imperceptiveness of his immediate physical surroundings as she and Stern made on the basis of his apparent lack of reaction to them, fail to take into account Lowry's extraordinary ability to absorb visual and aural data in an almost subliminal way, so that at times, when he appeared to have passed out from drinking, he could give an exact account of incidents that had happened when he seemed to be unconscious to the world. Lowry's physical antennae were extraordinarily highly developed.

In fact, as Hilda Thomas remarked in her essay on "Lowry's Letters" (*Malcolm Lowry: The Man and His Work*, ed. George Woodcock, 1971), one of Lowry's most attractive characteristics was his "humble regard for the natural world". Had we not learned to see him through *Under the Volcano* as par excellence the modern prose poet of damnation—a kind of flawed Dante—we would almost certainly be inclined to find a place for "The Forest Path to the Spring", with its accurate and limpid perceptions of wild life in its proper setting, beside the classic nature writing of such men as W. H. Hudson, H. D. Thoreau and Lowry's fellow adoptive Canadian Roderick Haig-Brown, as a work that reflects—even if with sometimes frightening ambiguity—a pantheistic sense of environment in which god, and devil as well, are wholly immanent. Paradise *exists* in such writings (it is only *hoped for* in *Under the Volcano*) and it is a paradise that can be apprehended directly through the senses, almost as if Lowry were following Ruskin's injunction, in *Modern Painters*, that "the whole power, whether of painter or poet, to describe rightly what we call an ideal thing, depends on its being thus, to him, not an ideal, but a *real* thing." But, like all paradises, that of "The Forest Spring", for all the almost pre-Raphaelite particularity with which it is presented to us, is precarious and its inhabitants are under perpetual threat of eviction (Lowry's habitual synonym for damnation). The hell that threatens, one is often led to assume, is what emerges out of man's non-physical life, out of the world of mind and soul. It is the fruit of the Tree of Knowledge as distinct from the Tree of Life.

> Half conscious I told myself [says the narrator of "The Forest Path . . ."] that it was as though I had actually been on the lookout for something on the path that had seemed ready, on every side, to spring out of our paradise at us, that was nothing so much as the embodiment in some frightful animal form of their nameless somnambulations, guilts, ghouls of past delirium, wounds to other souls and lives, ghosts of actions approximating to murder, even if not my own actions in this life. . . .

What Lowry means here is all that makes up the human *karma*, beyond and behind instinct, innocence and joy, insofar as it can be separated from the realm of nature.

Lowry's extreme sensitivity to place outside the mind can be seen if one considers the nature of the constant revision which he applied to the series of unfinished books on which he worked after completing *Under the Volcano*, in the hope of creating a great interlinking *chef d'œuvre*, "The Voyage that Never Ends", that would equal Proust's great masterpiece, *À la recherche du temps perdu*.

Proust of course, was as expert as Lowry at inducing in his readers a vivid multi-sensual apprehension of place. Lowry shares both spatial preoccupations and stylistic tricks with Proust, and one can make an interesting comparison between the French writer's treatment of the changing relationships of church spires seen from winding lanes near Combray in *Du côté de chez Swann* and Lowry's treatment in *Under the Volcano* of mountain peaks seen from a a circling Mexican hill road on the bus journey to Tomalín.

Indeed, there are passages of Lowry that read almost like pastiches of Proustian description, as in the early pages of *Under the Volcano*, when Jacques Laruelle—in Mexico—remembers with preternatural clarity the first time "he had seen, rising slowly and wonderfully and with boundless beauty above the stubble fields blowing with wild flowers, slowly rising into the sunlight, as centuries before the pilgrims straying over those same fields had watched them rise, the twin spires of Chartres Cathedral."

But there is an essential difference between Proust and Lowry in their treatment of place. Proust retreats to the cork-lined room of his final years, and what he presents through the voice of his namesake narrator is place conditioned by time and particularly by memory; that no experienced scene is ever so vivid as the involuntarily remembered scene is a central axiom of Proust's philosophy and of his method. His constant revision is aimed at making more perfect the presentation of scenes filtered through memory.

Lowry, on the other hand, was not concerned with conforming to the Platonic model offered by an irradiating and modifying memory of the past. He set out to draw significance from the experience of a lived present, and especially the lived present in a place that had acquired for him a peculiarly paradisial quality, the shores of Burrard Inlet at Dollarton, a few miles east of Vancouver and under the slopes of Seymour Mountain. The attempt to render that paradisial quality and exorcise its hellish counterpart in prose engaged and baffled him all the later years of his life. Only in one work, "The Forest Path to the Spring" did he wholly succeed in the task.

Lowry's attitude to place, and the ways he tried to express it, changed constantly from the beginning of his career. *Ultramarine* is a novel that seems subjective to the point of solipsism, yet even here place is an important element. One is aware of it not so much in the perfunctorily described harbours of the China Coast— "What did another port mean to him? Only another test of his steadfastness"—as in the vast spaces of ocean, so that a seaport evokes emotion only in night time stillness when one remembers the great waters beyond, as in the description of the *Oedipus Tyrannus* docking in Hong Kong harbour.

> But the sun spun round in its might towards the evening land of clouds, the atmosphere turned to evening with the burning of pale red stars—that night the *Oedipus Tyrannus* had reached another port, Hong Kong. She glided in silently at four bells in the evening. Lanterns were swinging at the water's edge, an army of lights marched with torches up the slope to the barracks, a few natives came aboard wearing enormous cymbal-shaped hats, but on the ship was dead silence, save for the hiss of the darkness. Oh God, oh God, if sea life were only always like that! If it were only the open sea, and the wind racing through the blood, the sea, and the stars for ever!

And, at the end of *Ultramarine*, in a passage whose imagery makes it read like a prose complement to James Elroy Flecker, the desert and the sea are equated as scenes of unending journey and search:

> . . . The Suez Canal! All around is the desert save where a cluster of palms struggle in the noonday fire; the eternal stream, which once was lost but lived always in the dreams of men. The anchor weighed, to be released, to glide slowly through the grey, sun-bleached land where the desert men kneel in still, confident peace, where the darkness draws in in a moment. Where the wild mysteries of the desert nights gleam in everything, in the sand garden's waste, in the palm's breath, in the starlight's cold, and in stars in motion on the dark stream. Then at last again to be outward bound, always outward, always onward, to be fighting always for the dreamt-of harbour, when the sea thunders on board in a cataract, and the ship rolls and wallows in the track of the frozen sea's storm. . . .

Place in *Ultramarine* is essentially unbounded space, the endless ways of the sea or the desert where the suffering immature spirit can at once escape from an unendurable present and continue into the future on the never-to-be-fulfilled Golden Journey of all youthful romantics who, like Flecker's pilgrims, search—

> Beyond that last blue mountain barred with snow,
> Across that angry or that glimmering sea. . . .

in the "lust of knowing what should not be known".

If *Ultramarine*, insofar as it is conceived in spatial terms, ends in a yearning for infinitely receding ocean or desert distances, *Under the Volcano* is dominated by the immuring mountain hori-

zons that form the physical correlative of the Consul's imprisonment in his private hell of destiny. Even that inner hell, too, is
seen—symbolically—in terms of space. In the never-delivered letter
to Yvonne that Laruelle finds between the pages of his dead friend's
Dr. Faustus, Geoffrey writes: "And this is how I sometimes think
of myself, as a great explorer who has discovered some extraordinary land from which he can never return to give his knowledge
to the world: but the name of this land is hell."

Under the Volcano is much closer than Lowry's later and un-
completed longer works of fiction to the conventional novels of
his time. The plot is elaborately structured; the characters are
fabricated out of observing many people instead of being merely
direct fictional projections of the author himself. And—which is
more germane to the subject of this essay—fictional place is
related closely to actual place, so that the imagined town of
Quahnahuac is made by grafting real-life Oaxaca on to real-life
Cuernavaca, in both of which Lowry lived out experiences remembered with an intensity which was more than Proustian, since
Lowry was never content with recollections but sought later to
relive the past, with the disastrous consequences reflected in *Dark
as the Grave Wherein my Friend is Laid* and the unpublished "La
Mordida", which tell what happened when he was drawn back to
the places out of which he had constructed the setting for *Under
the Volcano*.

When we turn to that novel, we see the special deliberateness
with which the landscape is used as a setting, in a cinematographic
rather than a theatrical sense. It is no static stage scene that we
perceive, for example, in the very first pages of the novel, when
—a year after the Consul's death—Jacques Laruelle, himself a
film-maker, looks out over the scene of his friend's last hours with
an eye as dispassionate as that of the universe itself. The knot of
mountains and their volcanoes is set in the mind's vision on the
world map, and then the focus narrows to the town of Quahnahuac,
and then to the tennis players, Laruelle and Dr. Vigil, sitting on
the terrace of the Hotel Casino de la Selva, and finally to Laurelle's
memory focusing the scene sharply on the Consul and his tragedy.

Thus we begin with a sense that place is vital to the novel, and
this sense never leaves us as we watch and live within the constantly varying scene of the last days in the Consul's journey to
damnation. There is no doubt that Lowry observed Mexico care-

fully, noted down his observations in the memorandum books he kept almost to his death, and retained a memory of his experiences exact and vivid enough to enable him to compose the final and successful version of *Under the Volcano* when he was already living in British Columbia, the *Paradiso* of his personal Divine Comedy. The terrain of Mexico had not only been seen; it had also been felt, in all its dramatic beauty, in all its latent menace. Had it not been felt in that way, its impact throughout the novel would not be so portentous, and we would not remember the novel so vividly in the mind's eye in the visual terms of people in an infernal landscape.

So we can assume that Lowry, in Mexico, responded intensely to Cuernavaca and Oaxaca as places—as natural and urban settings for the violent and death-obsessed Mexican way of existence, even before he decided to use them—in the brilliant cinematic manner he borrowed from the classic German film-makers— as the physical correlatives of his hero's inner experiences. The volcanoes, the neglected garden, the decaying palaces, the deep and dense *barranca*, are all more than mere features of a natural background. They reflect the Consul's inner condition— the own place of his mind—and in this way they force him into self-recognition and the reader into a dispassionate recognition of the Consul's condition. Yet at the same time they continue to be there objectively, just as Milton and Dante meant us to conceive the physical features of Hell objectively, and even as we try to isolate the symbolic elements of *Under the Volcano* we are forced to remember that this is the story of what happened in a material way to a man who dies. That man's inner life, for all its fancies and illusion, is nevertheless given its final expression in the foolish and sometimes splendid physical actions that end in his being shot and thrown into the *barranca* like a dead dog; in fact, with a dead dog. The Consul's hell may be internal, but the ministers of evil who kill him are part of the external Mexican world. The mind as its own subjective place can exist only in an objective place, and when the mind subjectively has gone into the hell of personal disintegration, then the outer world becomes hell too.

The constant interplay of human fantasy and of the fantasy of the external world, mind and matter perpetually reflecting each other, and manifested in such phenomena as coincidence and the near-coincidences Jung called synchronicity, always fascinated

Lowry. We can only understand *Under the Volcano* if we understand the kind of continuities or at least of correspondences that such a view implies. Mountain and *barranca* may symbolize the heaven and hell within the consul's heart, but they play their essential role in the novel—that of correlatives—only by being their solid selves: as solid, indeed, as symbols, if they are to be effective, must always become.

That Lowry used these elements of landscape—and of setting generally—quite deliberately and on several levels is clearly shown in the letter to his English publisher, Jonathan Cape, of 2 January 1946, which answered the readers' objections to the final version of *Under the Volcano* and preceded its final acceptance.

Lowry argues in this letter that the "Mexican local colour", whose abundance one of the readers criticized, is "all . . . there for a reason", and stresses the vital importance of his "use of Nature". When, later in the letter, Lowry describes the intent of the various chapters, the centrality of place to his concept and his structuring of the novel becomes quite evident. He maintains that the first chapter is necessary "more or less as it is, for the terrain, the mood, the sadness of Mexico", and, going into more detail, he continues:

> The scene is Mexico, the meeting place, according to some, of mankind itself, pyre of Bierce and springboard of Hart Crane, the age-old arena of racial and political conflicts of every nature, and where a colourful native people of genius have a religion that we can roughly describe as one of death, so that it is a good place, at least as good as Lancashire or Yorkshire, to set our drama of a man's struggle between the powers of darkness and light. Its geographical remoteness from us, as well as the closeness of its problems to our own, will assist the tragedy each in its own way. We can see it as the world itself, or the Garden of Eden, or both at once. Or we can see it as a kind of timeless symbol of the world on which we can place the Garden of Eden, the Tower of Babel and indeed anything else we please. It is paradisial; it is unquestionably infernal.

As we read on through the novel, with these hints from Lowry in our minds, we see that he not merely persists in laying on a thick *impasto* of vivid aural and visual detail, which accentuates the melodrama of the action in much the same way as the meticulous representation of incongruously gathered objects accentuates

119

the fantasy of a surrealist painting. He also carefully relates every-thing seen and heard and felt to the Consul's inner predicament which changes form as rapidly and dramatically as the views of volcanoes seen from the panning perspectives of the precipitous Mexican roads. And dominating the scene that is established with such portentous clarity in the imagination are the great mountains, which touch heaven and at the same time plunge their craters into the inner fires of the earth, and the great *barranca* and the dark wood, both linked specifically to the Dantesque inferno, and the dishevelled and neglected gardens—the Consul's own and those in public parks—which are the physical tokens of a lost paradise, even bearing their notices which the Consul interprets as threaten-ing the eviction of those who destroy them—a warning often to be reflected in his later writing.

The scape of wild nature which so persistently attracts our atten-tion in *Under the Volcano* must necessarily be shown as massive and spectacular and powerful if it is to bear the burden of the pre-ternaturally strong emotions which the various characters project on to it, often consciously, as reflections of their various natures, or perhaps more accurately of their various stages on the way of self-destruction. For the Consul it can be cruelly indifferent:

> The sun shining brilliantly now on all the world before him, its rays picking out the timberline of Popocatepetl as its summit like a gigantic surfacing whale shouldered out of the clouds again, all this could not lift his spirit. That sunlight could not share his burden of conscience, or sourceless sorrow. It did not know him.

It can also be diabolically complicitous:

> He lay back in his chair. Ixtaccihuatl and Popocatepetl, that image of the perfect marriage, lay now clear and beautiful on the horizon under an almost pure morning sky. Far above him a few white clouds were racing windily after a pale gibbous moon. Drink all morning, they said to him, drink all day. This is life!
> Enormously high too, he noted some vultures waiting, more graceful than eagles as they hovered there like burnt papers floating from a fire which suddenly are seen to be blowing swiftly upward, rocking.

And in the end it seems to preside with a knowing menace as the Consul, with drunkard's cunning, lightly but fatally puts the final touches to his half-conscious plot for his own destruction.

He was running, too, in spite of his limp, calling back to them crazily, and the queer thing was, he wasn't quite serious, running toward the forest, which was growing darker and darker, tumultuous above—a rush of air swept out of it, and the weeping pepper trees roared.

He stopped after a while; all was calm. No one had come after him. Was that good? Yes, it was good, he thought, his heart pounding. And since it was so good he would take the path to Parián, to the Farolito,

Before him the volcanoes, precipitous, seemed to have drawn nearer. They towered up over the jungle, into the lowering sky— massive interests moving up in the background.

For Hugh, on the other hand, retarded in adolescent romanticism, there is as he looks at the same landscape, a reaction that seems like an echo out of *Ultramarine* and Dana Hilliot's longing.

There was something in the wild strength of this landscape, once a battlefield, that seemed to be shouting at him, a presence born of that strength whose cry his whole being recognized as familiar, caught and threw back into the wind, some youthful password of courage and pride—the passionate, yet so nearly always hypocritical, affirmation of one's soul perhaps, he thought, of the desire to be, to do, good, what was right. It was as though he were gazing now beyond this expanse of plains and beyond the volcanoes out on the wide rolling blue ocean itself, feeling it in his heart still, the boundless impatience, the immeasurable longing.

And, a final example of the Mexican landscape reflecting states of mind and projecting as well as conspiring in destiny, there is the late passage describing part of the walk that Yvonne and Hugh take in search of the Consul.

They had reached the limit of the clearing, where the path divided into two. Yvonne hesitated, Pointing to the left, as it were straight on, another aged arrow on a tree repeated: *a la Cascada.* But a similar arrow pointed away from the stream down a path to their right: *a Parián.*

Yvonne knew where she was now, but the two alternatives, the two paths, stretched out before her on either side like the arms— the oddly dislocated thought struck her, of a man being crucified.

If they chose the path to the right they would reach Parián much sooner. On the other hand, the main path would bring them to the same place finally, and, what was more to the point, past, she felt sure, at least two other cantinas.

They chose the main path: the striped tents, the cornstalks dropped out of sight, and the jungle returned, its damp earthy leguminous smell rising about them with the night.

This path, she was thinking, after emerging on a sort of main highway near a restaurant-cantina named the Rum-Popo or the El Popo, took, upon resumption (if it could be called the same path), a short cut at right angles through the forest to Parián, across to the Farolito itself, as it might be the shadowy crossbar from which the man's arms were hanging.

The noise of the approaching falls was now like the awakening voices downwind of five thousand bobolinks in an Ohio savannah. Toward it the torrent raced furiously, fed from above, where, down the left bank, transformed into a great wall of vegetation, water was spouting into the stream though thickets festooned with convolvuli on a higher level than the topmost trees of the jungle. And it was as though one's spirit too were being swept on by the swift current with the uprooted trees and smashed bushes in débâcle towards that final fall.

Here, the features of the landscape project the themes of sacrifice/victimization and choice/free will, which are inevitably part of a novel so oriented towards damnation. The arrows are images of martyrdom and also signs offering a choice; the paths cross in ways that suggest to Yvonne on two separate occasions a crucifixion. The choice of paths leads one either to the Falls or to the Little Lighthouse, ironic source of light where the Consul will find darkness. But it is the path to the Falls that Yvonne takes, and the choice is underlined by the fact that miniature cascades are already plunging down beside them as they walk in the direction of the final fall towards which Yvonne feels her spirit being swept away. This of course is a premonitory image of the death that awaits her, but it is also a sign that this is a novel not only about eviction from paradise, but also about the Fall, in theological terms. And, of course, if anyone in the novel is unwilling victim and needless sacrifice, it is Yvonne.

Place in *Under the Volcano*, as manifested in the Mexican setting, is grandiose and indifferent or, subjectively seen, grandiose and menacing; the very scale of the natural phenomena intensifies the pettiness, the hopelessness, above all the eventual depersonalization of human endeavours, just as the scale of Dante's inferno emphasizes that ultimate wretchedness, beyond the human condition, beyond personality, in which its dwellers neither live nor truly die. As Lowry said of his Mexico: "It is paradisial; it is unquestionably infernal."

A paradise that was not infernal did find its way into the final, published version of *Under the Volcano*; the Consul, Yvonne and Hugh all think and talk of it, and we first encounter it in the Consul's letter which Laruelle finds in the copy of *Dr. Faustus* at the start of the novel:

> I seem to see us living in some northern country, of mountains and hills and blue water; our house is built on an inlet and one evening we are standing, happy in one another, on the balcony of this house, looking over the water. There are sawmills half-hidden by trees beyond and under the hills on the other side of the inlet, what looks like an oil refinery, only softened and rendered beautiful by distance.

Just before his fatal encounter with the neo-fascist vigilantes who kill him the Consul's thoughts turn again to that northern land so different from Mexico—and yet so similar in its cloud-topped mountains:

> British Columbia, the genteel Siberia, that was neither genteel nor a Siberia, but an undiscovered, perhaps an undiscoverable Paradise, that might have been a solution, to return there, to build, if not on his island, somewhere else, a new life with Yvonne. Why hadn't he thought of it before. Or why hadn't she?

And almost at the point of death one of Yvonne's last visions is of a northern house burning on a seashore: "Their house is dying, only an agony went there now."

Now, as anyone who has read the recent biographical literature on Lowry will know, he did find that "undiscovered, perhaps . . . undiscoverable Paradise", at Dollarton, British Columbia, which he called Eridanus in his later fiction; the view from his porch was that which the Consul envisaged, and his house burnt down, which led him in June 1944 to write a poetic "Lament", beginning with the lines: "Our house is dead / It burned to the ground / On a morning in June / With a wind from the Sound" and ending in the laconic words, significant in one who thought much of Hell, "But our home is gone. / And the world burns on."

From this time onwards a clear polarity of place appears in

123

Lowry's writing, related to a corresponding polarity of joy-and-despair, heaven-and-hell. If Mexico remains infernal, the paradisial is transferred to British Columbia and specifically to the foreshore at Eridanus, but the salvation which this paradisial place seems to assure is only conditional, and eviction always threatens its inhabitants, as it threatened—in the Consul's misreading of the Spanish noticeboards—those who entered the gardens of Mexico. The real, the material basis for this fear was that Lowry lived as a squatter on the foreshore, and was periodically threatened with expulsion by the harbour authorities; that threat corresponded to his haunting fear that the happiness and the creativity which he enjoyed at Dollarton were only temporary, a fear which he saw confirmed on the one occasion when he ventured back into Mexico, in 1945–46, and underwent a series of misadventures (described in his letters and in the biographies) in which that country appeared only in its infernal aspects.

The Dollarton-Mexico polarity appears in one way or another in almost all of Lowry's writings after *Under the Volcano*, though there is one book, "In Ballast to the White Sea", of which we know almost nothing, since it was destroyed in the fire that burnt Lowry's cabin in 1944.

Of the three unfinished novels that have survived, two—*Dark as the Grave where in my Friend is Laid* and the unpublished "La Mordida"—were based on the journey back to Mexico in 1945–46, when he failed to discover an old friend who he learnt had been killed in a drunken quarrel, when he himself became embroiled in difficulties with the immigration authorities which led to his being deported from the country, and when, to complete the psychic failure of the expedition, he allowed himself to sink into the morbid reliving of his first marriage, which collapsed in Mexico. He retained from this journey an even more negative picture of Mexico than he had created in *Under the Volcano*. Now it had become unrelievedly infernal, its paradisial aspects burnt away, its landscapes always threatening and its towns always sinister. It existed for him less as a memory than as an obsession, less as a place seen objectively in all its visual splendour than as Milton's hell in the own place of the mind.

But if Mexico had become all Inferno, then Eridanus-Dollarton, notably recorded in *October Ferry to Gabriola*, the remaining unfinished novel, and in "The Forest Path to the Spring" and other stories of *Hear Us O Lord From Heaven Thy Dwelling Place*, became in compensation all Paradise. In personal terms this was because, as Douglas Day has said in his *Malcolm Lowry*, it was "the only place where Lowry ever felt at ease, able to work, able to exercise some control over his drinking." It is true that there were other elements than that of place which contributed to the fugitive tranquillity, existing like a deep calm pool in the midst of the torrent of Lowry's life. The comparative success and stability of his second marriage, the withdrawn life among simple fishermen and boat builders, the occult studies he pursued under the old Golden Dawn devotee, "Frater Achad", all contributed, yet his letters and his last writings leave no doubt at all that this combination of fortunate circumstances would not alone have made Eridanus-Dollarton into a threatened paradise. The dominant element of place was needed, the world of nature that so dramatically and yet intimately surrounded him, the world in which he immersed himself both bodily and spiritually, the world of the tide that sucked under his floor-boards and the mountains that towered behind him, of the birds and cougars in the forest, of the killer whales and the gulls and the mergansers populating the sound in which he daily swam.

At Dollarton Lowry attained some interludes of peace, a fleeting sense of fulfilment, yet the consciousness of paradise has rarely on any level inspired great art, and whatever personal benefits Lowry may have gained from the years at Dollarton, the effect of the experience on his writing was mainly detrimental. It is probable that Lowry's life was prolonged by this interlude of relative happiness, but prolonged mostly for a succession of unresolved attempts at literary creation. Except in "The Forest Path to the Spring", Lowry never again achieved the extraordinary melding of place and person, of symbol and spirit, of the external world and the inner drama, of artist and artifact, that he had attained in *Under the Volcano*. In the end therapy took over from art, and in Lowry's last works the artist—in ways I shall shortly show—became more urgently important than his creations. Even therapy failed in the final, fatal weeks at Ripe, a third of a world and three years away from Dollarton, and Lowry's letters written during those final stages of his life illustrate the obsessional identification with place— at times the virtual identification of place and person—that characterized his attitude towards Dollarton.

Lowry and his wife Margerie had built a crazy, insecure pier to their squatter's cottage. It survived winter storms that knocked more solid structures awry, and in the end Lowry began to feel a peculiar affinity with this brave and fragile structure which seemed, like him, so threatened and yet so enduring. In the spring storms of 1956, by which time he had reached England, it was destroyed, and he learnt of its end in the summer of the same year with a sense of shock as if an old friend had died, as if the bell tolled now for him.

> I cannot believe our poor pier has been swept away: that pier that gave so much happiness to many and us, *was us* in a sense; . . . we risked our lives building it, and I am broken hearted it has gone.

The personalization of place seems to be carried even a step farther in the strange reference in one of Lowry's last letters—of 29 April 1957 to the Canadian poet Ralph Gustafson—to "the waterfront shack on Burrard Inlet which I still have that I loved or love more than life itself".

These references, made in the creatively barren last months of Lowry's life, might be dismissed as merely of biographical significance if they did not echo strikingly similar sentiments which are expressed by the central characters in two of the unfinished novels written at Dollarton. Sigbjørn Wilderness, travelling down to Mexico on his portentous journey in *Dark as the Grave wherein my Friend is Laid*, recalls with epiphanic intensity the first time he saw his first—since burnt—cabin in Eridanus, and remembers the later cabin as "their poor beloved rainy house in Eridanus, British Columbia". He remembers the great December storms that sweep up the inlet ("joyful, tremendous" yet at the same time fearful), and then it is "unbearable to think of their new little house, alone, in the sea, and unprotected", and only a few pages afterwards he sees "the unfinished house standing there helpless, all but unprotected, at the mercy of the shipwrecks, and battering weather, something indeed like their own lives".

Since Ethan Llewellyn, in *October Ferry to Gabriola*, is involved in the desperate search for a new home because he is threatened with eviction from Eridanus (a threat from which he is reprieved before the book ends), it is natural that memories of the inlet and the cabin, memories of the place, should be even more poignantly and extensively recorded than those of Wilderness in the other novel. And, indeed, we find him thinking that

> . . . their cabin seemed to possess a kind of life . . . that couldn't have been called forth wholly by its owners, or its past owners. One had come to love it like a sentient thing (and here it was more like a ship) with a life of its own, not that one just imagined as living, or that it flattered and amused one to consider doing so, because one had given it life oneself. . . . And the trouble was Ethan felt it still did live, after they'd abandoned it. . . . Well, this was animism certainly. . . .

And from this, Ethan comes to concluding:

> That among other things, between the cabin and themselves was a complete symbiosis. They didn't live in it, Ethan said, they wore it like a shell.

Such passages confirm one in the feeling that during the years at Dollarton Lowry not merely received a kind of physical therapy from the way he lived, but also that, on a less obvious level, his writing became a therapy after he completed *Under the Volcano*, so that he reversed the traditional progression of the novelist, which tends to be from the autobiographical to the invented. In his later work, in fact, Lowry was quite incapable of detaching his characters from himself or clearly distinguishing their experiences from his. Perilous as it is to identify any fictional character with a living person, it is difficult to avoid—in discussing *Dark as the Grave*—the admission that Sigbjørn Wilderness returning to Mexico *is* in a pecularly intimate way Malcolm Lowry following the same quest, and that Ethan Llewellyn and his wife setting off in *October Ferry* to find a home on Gabriola Island *are* likewise Lowry and his wife who undertook precisely the same quest for the same reason. *October Ferry* and *Dark as the Grave* are in fact failures both in fiction and in autobiography; Lowry is so possessed by his personal quests that his characters become unconvincing as fictional creations and also as projections of his inner self; there is an immense inhibition at the point of revelation, and episodes which one knows actually happened take on an air of unreal fantasy in these splendid failures of incomplete books.

It is, in fact, only in the visually live and stimulating descriptions of places—whether Mexican uplands or British Columbian coastland—that these books really detach themselves from their dominating and obsessive inhibitions and fears. Thus one can say that in his final phase Lowry's sense of *place* was stronger and truer than his sense of *person*, which as I suggested at the beginning of this essay, places him among the poets of damnation and salvation, who wrote of a realm where personality had reached its end.

This is what makes it appropriate that "The Forest Path to the Spring", that slight novella in which the leading character is so neutrally sketched that we cannot even clearly define him as a persona of Lowry, in which the action is shifted away from a melodramatic Lowrian search for an impossible grail into a flimsy plot of psychic experiences while carrying water through a wood to a foreshore cabin, should assume in Lowry's later career the role of key work which *Under the Volcano* assumes in his earlier career. The reason why it makes its special appeal, why it seems uniquely successful and consummated among Lowry's later works, is precisely that it has admitted and accommodated his growing sense of the precedence of *place*—including "own place"—over *person*.

From the very opening lines—"At dusk every evening, I used to go through the forest to the spring for water"—a tone is set, and the characters and the action are quietened as the picture of a place and the fragile way of human existence that exists within it are created. Out of that creation emerges a sense of unity with nature, in its destructive as well as its regenerative aspects, as near the paradisial as Tartarus-haunted Lowry came.

> And the rain itself was water from the sea, as my wife first taught me, raised to heaven by the sun, transformed into clouds, and falling again into the sea, while within the inlet itself the tides and currents in that sea returned, became remote, and becoming remote, like that which is called the Tao, returned again as we ourselves had done.

If we think of *Under the Volcano* as Lowry's Paradise Lost, "The Forest Path to the Spring" is his Paradise Regained, and it is appropriate that, like the original Paradise Regained, it should be both briefer and less dramatically striking than its Satanic counterpart. But, as in Milton's great epics, *place* is essential. Heaven and Hell are to be conceived, in Ruskin's terms, as *real* before they can be ideally apprehended, and this happens in Lowry's magical forest harbouring the spring of salvation as much as in his shadowing volcanoes that preside over damnation. In the classic cosmogonies Hell and Paradise had their fixed and proper and actual places. One must be able to locate the *own place* of the mind as surely as these other places, and in his two most fully achieved works Lowry does it.

6

"The Forest Path to the Spring":
An Exercise in Contemplation

by PERLE EPSTEIN

Like Faust, Malcolm Lowry always found himself with his eyes on heaven and one foot in hell. In his life as in his work, Lowry never managed to emerge successfully from *Under the Volcano*, the intended "inferno" portion of a projected seven-novel saga, a twentieth-century *Divine Comedy*. "The Forest Path to the Spring", a novella contained in a collection of stories called *Hear Us O Lord From Heaven Thy Dwelling Place*, represents the hopeful beginning of the path to paradise. In this lyrical prose-poem, Lowry, in the persona of a jazz musician, regenerates his fallen spirit through the medium of Nature. Little actually happens in the way of plot; indeed, upon close reading the entire story reveals itself as a stage-by-stage depiction of one man's meditation. References to Taoism, Buddhism, Swedenbørg proliferate, pointers along the path of this unorthodox mystic who, like the Consul in *Under the Volcano*, harbours messianic visions which plunge him into the depths from which he must withdraw the holy sparks. The job, however, is too much for him, and our nameless jazz musician is barely extricated with his soul intact by Nature, in the guise of his loving wife.

The prodigal Everyman and his Eve come to British Columbia on their honeymoon and decide to stay on despite the primitive conditions that prevail on the little inlet called *Eridanus*, a typically Lowrian three-tiered metaphor: the name of a decaying shipwrecked steamer, with its shipload of "cherries in brine" to remind them of the bittersweet fruit on the tree of life; a heavenly constellation to guide them higher; and the name of one of the rivers of Paradise, simultaneously referred to as the "River of Life"

130

and the "River of Death", reflecting the double-edged nature of the path to the Absolute.

For anyone who has ever sat down to practise some form of disciplined meditation (as Lowry did under the guidance of one Frater Achad, a self-styled "Christian Cabbalist", otherwise British Columbian census-taker, who enrolled the Lowrys in his meditation course after being asked in for a drink), "The Forest Path to the Spring" is a familiar recounting of the boredom, fear, restlessness, self-confrontation, anger and hopeless doubt confronted along the way. Meditation is usually performed twice daily, at dawn and at dusk. Lowry's jazz musician, under the guidance of his wife, learns to meditate on Nature as he awakens—both literally and figuratively—to its powers of renewal. In this fashion, the earthbound artist strives to find his lost innocence by cleansing himself of a corrupt civilization, literally plunging into the waters each morning and washing away the grime of the cities of dreadful night which he had inhabited for so long. Training himself gradually to see daylight for the first time, sleeping at night and rising with the sun, the jazz musician becomes worthy of making the trip through the forest at dusk every evening to fetch water from a mountain spring.

Now physically fit as a result of his new bodily disciplines, the meditator is ready to wander through Dante's sacred wood—that traditional symbol of the human psyche, with mountains surrounding him on one side, the ocean's depths on the other, planted on the narrow path (as narrow, say the Hindu mystics, as the edge of a razor)—ready to confront his own churlishness and fear, which always threaten "to spring out of our paradise . . . those nameless somnambulisms, guilts, ghouls of past delirium . . . ready to leap out and destroy me".

The "dawn", or early phase of concentrated awareness is sometimes perceived as a "white fire", at other times as "chaos". Frequently, one finds oneself in places where wolves howl in an everlasting night, and where "Chinese poems" are scrawled across the face of the moon. So the setting provides an extended nature metaphor, or series of nature metaphors, of the imagination preparing itself for deep contemplation. To compound the meditative setting, Lowry describes his hero's little shack and those of his neighbours as "monastic cells of anchorites or saints". Then, in a humorous light, the obverse side of the hermetic life, those same shacks are called "Dunwoiken" and "Hi-Doubt". The final outpost, the shack nearest the mountains, is called "Four Bells". (Zen meditation, for example, is begun and completed to the sound of bells rung twice at each sitting.)

The meditation enclosure is surrounded on two sides by access to the outside world: a railroad line, and boats bobbing in the inlet. The city is "invisible", behind him on the path, for the contemplative must, at least for the period of his retreat, turn his back on the city and all it stands for, ambition, striving, wealth and mercantile enterprises, which Lowry embodies in images of "cantilever bridges, skyscrapers and gantries of the city. . . ." At the southern tip of the enclosure a "magic" lighthouse sheds its "beneficent" beams. The northernmost point in the line of the mountains is called "Paradise" by the local Indians. Thus delineated, the externalized quarters of the narrator's mental environs allow him to examine his own responses to the sheer inactivity of extended self-exploration. The little cottage located even further north than "Four Bells" is therefore called *Wywurk*, a question that mocks and irritates the meditator who always asks himself, "What am I doing here?" when he finds himself cut off from the "normal" stimuli of the everyday world. Hurriedly erected by temporary residents, shacks like *Wywurk* strike the narrator as existing only by the grace of the Harbour Board, "upon whom I often felt must have sat God Himself". Part-time monastics who come to refresh themselves each summer by bathing in the paradisical waters, he finds hard to tolerate in his no-nonsense commitment to the path. Permanent dwellers, however, like the "abbot" of the inlet, a Manx boatbuilder of few words, who, not unlike an unpredictable Japanese *roshi*, bursts into song and performs kind deeds for his "monks" in secret, guide the novice toward the "light". Also like Zen monks, the small group of fishermen who populate the inlet go out to earn their keep at sea, or in the city, only returning when the temporary people have gone, appropriately enough, after "Labour Day". During storms the fishermen protect even the abandoned shacks of the temporary dwellers in Paradise, wordlessly, as fishers of men who tend to the bodies and souls of even the most unworthy and inattentive apostles. Sam the lighthouse "monk", is engaged in a perpetual hymn of praise to Nature; he is unfallen Adam, naming and glorifying all things at once.

The enclosure, surrounded as it is by the twin paths of Life and

Death (the two streams flowing forth from Eridanus), is a perpetual reminder of the musician's own tenuous connexion with
Paradise: "a condemned community perpetually under the shadow
of eviction". The meditator must carefully pick his way along the
path, suspended between life and death, peace and hell—the
latter, vividly defined by a demonic, fire-belching oil refinery. But
having come that far, past the first "honeymoon" week, the narrator cannot look back. Such total commitment immediately in-
duces fear; the first encounter with Eridanus therefore bears for
him "the quality of a nightmare". The seven Scotsmen who are
to rent him their cabin sit in a cloud of steaming heat with the
woodstove burning, cackling over a bubbling mutton broth, like a
group of crazy Zen monks testing the fortitude of the probationer
at the gate of their monastery. Entering Eridanus, the contemplative plane, is like being thrown into the paradoxical world of the
mischievous examiner-monks who seem to be doing everything
wrong in order to test the sincerity of the petitioner at their gates.
The disorienting experience is cast in a veil of illusion which presents the first glimpse of Paradise as a hellish, malodorous polluted
beach, populated by noisy bathers who squawk in a babel of
tongues.

For the tenacious novice, however, the pristine nature of Paradise is revealed the next day when the beach is miraculously
divested of the crowds and dirt. The young couple, having passed
the test of worthiness, now immerse themselves in the water.
"After that we swam sometimes three and four times a day." Like
the primordial Adam and Eve, they examine their island. Humbled
by the sight of the railroad-line dwellings which actually permit
a view of the mountain ranges in their entirety, the narrator learns
that only the truly meek, the "poorest" people in Eridanus, are
allowed total vision. Only by eliminating his egoistic perception of
the world may the seeker transcend dualism and stop "the opposing motions born of the motion of the earth", the "symbol" of
"illusion".

The initial dip into Paradise takes place while a war rages in
the "real" world without. Is the serenity an illusion? muses the
narrator, a short-lived and selfish denial of the tragedy raging
beyond the waters of Eridanus? To confirm that this stage of his
life is indeed an *Intermezzo*, a canoe bearing that name mysteriously surfaces from the water, another warning on a path strewn

with deliberately symbolic yardsticks that point to the obstacles he will have to overcome. The "honeymoon", the canoe informs him, cannot last forever. One of the first precepts of Buddhism, for instance, is the realization of the impermanence of all things. The Tao is ever flowing, as he notes at various points in the story. Threats of Paradise Lost therefore hover over the ghosts of other lovers long since separated. Eridanus turns its darker face upward and becomes the river Styx. The hero has been allowed his respite in order to get his ailing body and mind into shape for the great effort to come, the real confrontation in the wilderness of the Self. Like the true yogi who has decided to spend more than a mere summer's vacation at the job, the musician must strip himself of attachment to external comforts and accept the ascetic conditions that prevail in the forest. "Lack of plumbing, oil lamps, no ordinary comforts of any kind in the cold weather . . . to live here . . . would be almost tantamount, I thought, to renouncing the world altogether. . . ." But he is nonetheless struck by an overwhelming tide of "love" at the thought of the task (the true mystic's armour against doubt and fear) when he sees the shack in a new light, "as much a part of the natural surroundings as a Shinto temple is of the Japanese landscape", that is, as his spiritual home.

The passing of summer into fall, and then into winter (entering undifferentiated states of consciousness, emptiness) brings with it further tests of the meditator's stamina. Against the cold whiteness of the November snow, the stark loneliness of the forest, he recalls as he peers at his own shadow cast upon the white frost exactly why he is standing there in the first place, enduring "the glowering embodiment of all that threatened us; yes, even a projection of that dark, chaotic side of my self, my ferocious destructive ignorance". Gradual progress along the mystical path is certain to bring with it the realization of one's "ignorance", of how little one truly knows about life, Nature, God, the cycle of the Tao. Yet, at this seemingly hopeless admission of ignorance, one acknowledges, too, that love will provide a "continual awakening", and the essential fortitude to withstand the onslaughts of fear which threaten to paralyse further progress on the path. Here, the musician's young wife provides him with the courage to go on. He comes home every day to her after only twenty minutes' separation like a traveller who has been long and far away.

All the secrets of Nature, say the mystics, are revealed to the patient seeker who is willing to separate himself from distraction in order to contemplate her. Some systems advocate contemplation of the smallest organic forms—a snail or a flower—as an entry into investigating oneself. Working from the outside in, as it were, the narrator learns from the snow and the fire, the violent tides that uproot trees and threaten to shake his home from its moorings, of the "eternal movement, and eternal flux and change, as mysterious and multiform in its motion and being, and in the mind as the mind flowed with it. . . ." After realizing experientially that the flux of mind and nature are one, that life is, in fact, ever-changing, that thoughts race like the tide, he achieves a moment of stillness, and with it a brief insight into the eternal and unchanging field against which the flickering events take place—what "the Chinese call the Tao, that, they say, came into existence before Heaven and Earth, something so still, so changeless, and yet reaching everywhere, and in no danger of being exhausted. . . ." Soon everything, even the apparently inanimate rocks dividing him from the water, throb with life, with pantheistic energy, "each bearing the name of a divinity". Once in accord with Nature, he is provided by her with the necessary implements for his ascent into still higher levels of awareness: the beach mysteriously produces an old ladder that, when refurbished, allows him to climb onto the path.

One morning the couple notice a "new" sunrise. Gleaming like the lighthouse beam, it picks out an old cannister, a grail of sorts, covering it in "silver light", beckoning the musician to pick it up, clean it, and use it to fetch fresh water from the mountain source, his most significant "chore" to date. Appropriately, the Danish Mr. Kristbjorg (Christ Mountain?) appears, points out their "wand" (a Danish word for "water"), and initiates the musician into the way, "not a hundred yards from the house, though we hadn't seen it". Kristbjorg, guardian of the path to the spring, "had waved a magic wand and suddenly, there was the water".

The trip to the source, however, must be made alone. The narrator notes how vivid every colour, tree and star appear, how the "moon" comes and goes, all metaphorical descriptions of the various visual phenomena which occur during concentration. Sufimystics even designate one particular stage of concentration as

135

"seeing the moon"; the Japanese mystic calls it "seeing one's own face". Coming back in a "blue fog" from that faraway place that is really only twenty minutes away, the narrator readjusts to the world of everyday reality, and, grateful that he is able to return, finds solace in the homely touches his wife has added to the shack: the curtains and the "full lamplight inside". Return to love and human kinship, to "ordinary" life, is a necessary relief from the eerie experience of examining the mental "forest".

As he grows more acquainted with the path, the musician develops a "system" for approaching the spring:

> First I climbed the wooden ladder. . . . Then I turned right so that now I was facing north toward the mountains, white plumaged . . . or rose and indigo.
>
> Often I would linger on the way and dream of our life. Was it possible to be so happy?

Chinese Taoist meditation sketches just such visualized routes for achieving one-pointedness. Here, the narrator's physical actions seem to overlap with this type of visualization exercise. And, true to meditative form, the deeper the silence, the more terrifying the eruption of deep-seated emotion:

> Returning homeward along the path, I found myself possessed by the most violent emotion I had ever experienced in my life . . . so all-embracingly powerful it made me stop in my tracks and put my burden down . . . I had been thinking how much I loved my wife, how thankful I was for our happiness, then I had passed to thinking about mankind, and how this once innocent emotion had become . . . hatred.

Most frequently this upsurge of hatred, or anger, or lust, etc. is experienced physically; here it "throbs" in his blood, makes his "hair stand on end. . . ." The meditator plods on nonetheless, continuing "homeward", but the experience of the emotion is so great that he is stopped from time to time by the recurring bouts of sheer undisguised hatred for mankind that consume him. Personified in the image of a blazing forest fire, "my hatred became a thing in itself, the pattern of destruction." And, like the forest fire that doubles back on itself after destroying everything in its path, the hatred "turns back on itself, to devour my very self in its flames". For the ego can only be annihilated by the purgative flames of self-confrontation. Such visions, say the Buddhists, are embodied mental projections of every secret residing within the mind—hence, the personified "devils" of Mara's army which attacked the Buddha during his forest meditation, where wrath and hatred are depicted as a god with flaming hair who shoots flaming arrows.

But the musician is chastened by the loving thought of his decent neighbours, the fishermen, who always help him to repair his falling house, bring him food, those fellow forest dwellers who are not as "shiftless" as he is, more experienced anchorites who have long since tamed their passions. He compares them to "benevolent mountain lions", images of the conquered ego, and the wrath which he too will learn to tame when a living mountain lion turns up in his path one day. As if echoing his own thoughts, the kindly Scotsman who mends the door of the narrator's house, reminds him with his little song that:

> You've got a long way to go
> You've got a long way to go
> Whether you travel by day or night. . . .

The guardians of the path can only take a man so far; the rest remains for his wife to teach him—"tenderness . . . compassion . . . capacity for delight". Once again, love is able to draw him back from the frozen snows of isolation and the blazing flames of hatred into the human community, thereby strengthening him for his "chore".

Through performance of the physical tasks necessary for his survival, he finds himself capable of song, "as if we had discovered the primitive beginnings of music again for ourselves". The natural rhythms of the forest meet with the natural rhythms of the human body and express themselves through music. Now he need no longer run from his old life; he can incorporate his past, even respect it without ruminating over it or cursing it. The natural expression of music, the harmony of body and mind are translated into "work"; as one immensely practical Zen master noted: *One who does no work for a day does not eat for a day.* Having integrated past and present, the jazz musician may return to action, use his talent, make money from it, and simultaneously cleanse himself of doubt and hatred by means of his contribution to the human community. Work, too, informs him that he will inevitably return to "the city", that the forest is only a respite for a musician, an

Intermezzo from which he must learn in order to return with love to the "mankind" he had once so despised.

Though "continually possessed by the uprush of his extraneous thoughts", the meditator plunges still deeper into himself. Having withstood the devastating winter thunderstorms that echo his tumultuous thoughts, he wakes up one day to find with "pride that one had survived, the sense of life, the fear of death. . . ." The inner battles have perhaps been fiercer than the outer storm. Having learned how to plunge *into* the tumult rather than to escape from it (compare the Zen exercise which advises one to go *with*, and not *away* from pain), he wants "to dive swiftly into that brimming sea to acquire a greater appetite still, either that or because the sea seemed safer than the house". At this point, the once protective house, the homely comfort and warmth of everyday life, may be discarded in favour of the leap into non-duality.

In taming his own wildness, the narrator even comes to tame the animals along his path; wild birds no longer fly away at his approach, but accept food from his hand and respond to his call. One consequence of meditation, according to Patanjali, a Hindu mystic, is an acquaintance with the language of the birds and beasts. Solomon, for example, could "talk" to animals; while numerous stories have been circulated about yogis who tame wild tigers with a mere salute. (Lowry probably parodies these legends intentionally in the serio-comic meeting with the mountain lion.)

One day the musician experiences a brief flash of illumination (*satori*, epiphany) as he treads the path while meditating on a break in a jazz tune by trumpeter Bix Beiderbecke. Urged by the experience to "do something good" (which, for the artist is synonymous with *creating* something), he is prompted to "translate this happiness" into music. And, just as suddenly, he grows fearful lest in trying to fasten the spiritual moment to the material world he will accomplish something evil. (*Thou shalt not make graven images.*) But he is saved from his fear of coarsening the ineffable by the intercession of myth. The first man to clear the forest path to the spring, he learns, was named Proteus; the current inhabitant of the shack along the path is named Bell; hence the "Proteus-Bell Path". This odd conjunction leads the narrator to reflect on the Blakean reality of myth, the interdependence of the sense world (which, since Locke and Descartes, is believed to be the only reality) and the world of creative imagination populated by gods, celestial beings, animated rocks and talking birds. "How mysterious! . . . Were we living a life that was half real, half fable?" The meditator, opening up to the myriad planes of "reality", suddenly becomes aware of the coincidences, or correspondences between the physical and imaginal realms. "Did the confusion", he muses, "come from pinning the labels of one dimension on another? Or were they inextricable?" Indeed, only in art can the numerous dimensions be properly identified. So, prompted to recreate his "illumination" in humanly communicable terms, he begins to compose a symphony.

Despite the one encouraging flash, however, the narrator is compelled to return again and again to his chore. "And then, before I had time to think, I would seem to be getting water again, walking as if eternally through a series of dissolving dusks down the path. And at last the night would come like a great Catherine wheel." Time is lost during deep contemplation; the wheel is associated with the inexorable wheel of the Law, whose very rotation is the tie between one dimension and another. As if mirroring the circular motions of the wheel himself, the narrator again reaches the place of fear, this time embodied in anxiety over losing his Isle of Delight. Realizing that the hermitage must be absorbed as a state of mind rather than as a physical place to which he can flee in escape from the world, he confronts his childish longing for the ideal sanctuary, "where one feels neither cold nor heat, nor sadness nor sickness of body or soul. . . . What if I should lose it?"

Then spring comes, and with it the breakthrough. When he looks, smells, and is absorbed by Nature, he forgets his fear—only to find something worse in its place. "I . . . found myself to my surprise not looking at anything nor smelling anything. And now, all of a sudden, very different seemed the journey back." The cannister grows heavy, his feet slip, his breath comes short. This is the phase of meditation where the task becomes unbearable. "And now I stopped and cursed my lot." Monstrous phenomena suddenly appear to lure him to suicide; he broods over his inevitable expulsion from the garden; the ladder becomes "the past, up and down which one's mind every night meaninglessly climbs!" He has reached the dead end point where the present moment is sacrificed to aimless preoccupation with the past, and fearful projection into the future. The chore grows "heavy" with thought.

This usually occurs immediately after a high phase of contemplation signaled by ecstatic self-satisfaction, like the experience which
had prompted the musician to compose his symphony. Paradoxically, it is by hitting bottom that he prepares himself for the most
significant confrontation of all.

Plodding along in his disgruntled state, he sees a cougar rest-
ing in a tree; Blake's *tyger*, a manifestation of all the obstacles
to enlightenment combined. "It was as though I had entered the
soul of a past self . . . mysteriously the lion was all that too."
The beast gazes at him; yogilike, the narrator speaks to it; the
cougar leaves and, we later learn, is killed by a fearless trapper who
loses a chunk of arm in the process. The bizarre event frees the
narrator of his past, allows him to venture forth the next night,
unburdened of his fear, to perform his chore. "I was only conscious
of the hill when I realized that I had traversed it without effort."
The gloomy thoughts of before, he now sees "at a distance, as if
below me". Objective observation of the nature of one's thoughts
marks a real meditative victory. Lowry sums up the experience
perfectly: "thoughts flowed, they were like a river, an inlet, they
comprised a whole project impossible to recapture or pin down.
Nonetheless those thoughts, and they were abysmal, not happy as
I would have wished, made me happy in that though they were in
motion they were in order too. . . . I was aware that some horrendous extremity of self-observation was going to be necessary to
fulfill my project." The creation of a symphony, i.e. the har-
monic organization of the otherwise chaotic buzz that comprises
"thought", will represent, in the outer world, the moment of illumination.

> Dear Lord God, I earnestly pray you to help me order this work,
> ugly, chaotic and sinful though it may be . . . thus so it seems
> to my imperfect and disordered brain . . . please help me to
> order it, or I am lost. . . .

This plea for grace, the stage of total self-surrender to a higher
force, enables the musician to let go of his stultifying ego and
enables him to "die through it, without dying of course, that I
might become reborn".

Gradually shedding his ego, the musician finds that the path on
his way back from the spring is virtually shorter each day. As
though " 'a great burden had been lifted off my soul.' I had a con-

sciousness of a far greater duration of time having passed during which something of vast importance to me had taken place, without my knowledge and outside time altogether." This aptly marks the moment of *satori*, the timeless, selfless, non-logical experience of pure consciousness. Like Camus' *Sisyphus*, whose stone-rolling provides him with his existential *raison d'etre*, Lowry's musician, by engaging with his chore, finds his ticket to enlightenment. Thoughts of suicide give way to the urge to create, and the eventual composition of a successful opera, "suggested probably by my thoughts of cleansing and purgation and renewal". Now he actually identifies with the "mystical" experience. As it pertains to self-knowledge, the chore becomes light, the path shorter; indeed, it threatens to disappear altogether—along with the ego which disappears in his "desire to be a better man, to be capable of more gentleness, understanding, love—"

Lowry's narrator describes his experience as a "blinding light . . . so that I seemed to contain the reflected sun deeply within my very soul . . .", the most common metaphor for illumination in all traditions. And, like other mystics, having relinquished his false identification with his past, the narrator becomes a channel for the music and creation comes easily. The "baptism" which follows, depicted by a dip in the water, is continued when the house burns down in a fire with all his music in it; the baptisms by water and fire completed, he is able to rebuild both the house and the symphony.

Seen years later, the house becomes the outward symbol of "ramshackle impermanence", of "improvisation"—yet emblematic of a "beauty of existence" which includes all the contradictions that constitute living: "Longing and hope . . . loss and rediscovery, failure and accomplishment", the list of polarities which must be reconciled in order to complete the chore of self-observation. Like a "blind man recovering his sight", with his wife as his guide, he had first opened his eyes to the world of daylight, stars, flowers, nature. Then, to the world of the "inner ear". On returning to Eridanus years after the initial event, the musician reflects on that time when he had been "living at the edge of eternity" in meditation on the forest path. Now the sound of bells seems to confirm his "great spiritual victory of mankind", tolling in honour of the private act of liberation that occurred there.

"The significance of the experience lay not in the path at all," he reflects, "but in the possibility that in converting the very can-nister I carried, the ladder down which I climbed every time I went to the spring—in converting both these derelicts to use I had pre-figured something I should have done with my soul." Here the musician echoes the sentiments of the yogis who claim that one must frequently use a thorn to remove a thorn, that only by utilizing our very weakness, the limited and ruminating mind, can we surpass it and find our untarnished selves.

The hero of this story, unlike the fallen Consul of *Under the Volcano*, comes to understand the need for freeing himself of the "tyranny of the past", and learns "that it was my duty to trans-cend it in the present". Facing the past "without fear", looking the lion in the eyes, as it were, he is able to create his symphony, as well as his life. Confronting the past with "clawbar and hammer", as he describes the meditative experience, for a "supernatural end", the musician sees beyond the words which merely symbolize things—"spring", "water", "tides", "deer", experiencing the *things in themselves* in the freshness of the present, minus the overlay of past fears or future fantasies; his is the immediate ex-perience of reality "beyond that symbolized or reflected" in the shadows of Plato's cave.

The narrator's final metaphorical reflection of his *satori* ex-perience echoes the *Upanishads*, which also describe man's life as "a drop falling into the sea, each producing a circle in the ocean, or the medium of life itself, and widening into infinity, though it seems to melt into the sea, and become invisible, or disappear entirely, and be lost". One with the Tao at last, with the rain "that itself was water from the sea", living, returning, dying, re-turning, "as we ourselves had done . . ." like "that which is called the Tao" is the great lesson of the journey along the forest path to the spring, which is itself that Taoist symbol of coursing life "on its last lap to the sea". The musician and his wife stoop and drink of the waters of life, which, for Lowry, only assumes signifi-cance in difficult, sometimes unbearable situations, places inhabited by the poor, the dispossessed, even in hell itself.

Whether he lives in a Rousseauean forest hut, rises at dawn among the beggars and outcasts of the Farolito, or locks him-self willingly in an insane asylum, the seeker must cut himself off from ordinary life in order to find his way back into himself. Lowry's characters deliberately lower themselves into the abyss of the world's agony so that the flame of "mystical illumination" will burn all the brighter. But at least here, in "The Forest Path to the Spring", the goal is achieved.

NOTES

1 Quotations taken from *Hear Us O Lord From Heaven Thy Dwelling Place* (Phila., 1961).

7

Intention and Design in "October Ferry to Gabriola"

by M. C. BRADBROOK

New light has been thrown on the later work of Malcolm Lowry by the MSS drafts for *October Ferry to Gabriola*, now deposited at the University of British Columbia by Mrs. Lowry; by the return of notebooks that had been lent to his biographer, and by the acquisition through Dr. Sherrill Grace of a copy of "Work in Progress"—over sixty pages of typescript, sent to his agent by Lowry in 1951, and forwarded to Albert Erskine, Lowry's editor.[1]

Taken together, these reinforce the view that Lowry sought a new form which did not lend itself to conventional issue in print. It lies between oral forms of the ballad or the seaman's yarn, with their multiple unstable versions, and radical new forms, such as the "neo-Gothic novel" in England, the *nouveau roman* in France. Alain Robbe-Grillet wrote:

> One of the most striking features of the new novel is a different attitude towards the reader, who is required to co-operate with the writer in constructing a world open to extension by the reader's imagination; he is no longer offered a fictional world that is 'complete', finished and closed in upon itself.[2]

Mrs. Lowry testified in a note that Lowry did not expect all the allusions in *Under the Volcano* to be recognized; but "they were present in the collective unconscious of Europe". Successive drafts changed them, as in the work of Joyce; but Lowry would also accept from Earle Birney or Maurice Nadeau an interpretation which had not occurred to him; as he said to David Markson "It is equally *your* book."[3] The text was never final—as Nadeau knew "*Lowry, lui, autorise toutes les interprétations et en sugère quelques autres.*" His long defence of *Under the Volcano* described

144

many structural possibilities: "It can even be regarded as a sort of machine: it works, too, believe me, as I have found out" he wrote to Jonathan Cape (*Selected Letters*, p. 66). Energy must be put into a machine to make it work; it will perform differently under different conditions.

From the first, Lowry had built with short units that, taken together, complemented each other. As early as 1940 he had written to James Stern:

> It is possible to compose a satisfactory work of art by the simple process of writing a series of good short stories, complete in themselves, good if held up to the light, water-tight if held up-side down, but full of effects and dissonances that are impossible in a short story, nevertheless having its purity of form, a purity that can be achieved only by the born short story writer.
>
> (*Selected Letters*, p. 28)

This is best shown in the collection *Hear Us O Lord*; and although in "Work in Progress" Lowry said he wanted to write something "as simple as a daisy", a daisy is a composite flower.

The metaphor of the machine is continued by implication in an important quotation taken from Ortega y Gasset in a letter dated 30 June 1950:

> In the vacuum arising after he (i.e. Man) has left behind his animal life he devotes himself to a series of non-biological occupations which are not imposed by nature but invented by himself. This invented life—invented as a novel or play is invented— man calls "human life", well-being. It is not given to man as its fall is given to a stone. . . . He makes it himself, beginning by inventing it. . . . Is man a sort of novelist of himself who conceives the fanciful figure of a personage with its unreal occupations and then, for the sake of converting it into reality, does all the things he does—and becomes an engineer?
>
> (*Selected Letters*, p. 210)

In the early drafts of *October Ferry*, the protagonist, Ethan Llewelyn, was an engineer, though afterwards, as a lawyer, he was engaged in constructing more social edifices. A story, dropped from the collection *Hear Us O Lord*, entitled "In the Black Hills" tells of a German mining engineer who came to a little town, drank deeply but made no friends, was found dead and charitably given a pauper's funeral by the simple narrator of the tale, clubbing with a few others. Yet as the German sought oblivion and found it, his life was not devoid of glory. "In those days, a man could get away somewhere." This tale answers one of the questions in the Notebooks—"What do you seek? Oblivion." (It is now printed in *Psalms and Songs* [New York, 1975].)

October Ferry is based upon an actual journey taken by the Lowrys in October 1946, in search of a new home, since their water-side shack might be razed. "The difficulty of the future taking any shape at all, as of the present having any meaning for the protagonist is really the whole plot" Lowry confided of *October Ferry* to Albert Erskine, in an unpublished letter; his editor in reply wonders if it isn't all depth, and if "all these themes are being communicated with enough purely narrative and surface interest".[4]

Lowry's form was not apparent to this sympathetic reader, but it was not purely subjective. The concern with pollution and despoilment of the environment was ahead of its time; today its significance is plain. The Gothic novel, which Lowry had been studying (he dates some of his letters from "The Castle of Otranto") has since been revived in the work of John Fowles, *The Magus*. Combination of the two strands may be detected in the very widely acclaimed novels of Margaret Atwood, particularly in *Surfacing* (1972), in which a return to the Indian wilderness of Canada and the buried self is presented through a surrealist journey. The enemy is the advertiser, the brash visitor from south of the border; wilderness and the sense of identity blend into one.

Novels have since Lowry's time been published in loose-leaf form, so that the reader may rearrange the chapters to suit himself. Lowry left behind for *October Ferry* a mass of MSS and memoranda, which Mrs. Lowry sorted, cut and edited into the published version. "Professionally, we are dealing with corrupt texts" austerely observed the editor of *Dark as the Grave*, Douglas Day. (An earlier work, known as *Lunar Caustic*, exists in three versions, and in an unpublished letter of 11 January 1952, Lowry asked Giroux to print all three.) The original short story out of which grew *October Ferry* was submitted to *Harpers* as by Malcolm Lowry and Margerie Bonner. Mrs. Lowry defended herself against the charge that she was introducing her own words into *Dark as the Grave*:

> I think it is ridiculous. I certainly wrote plenty of lines and scenes when I was editing "The Forest Path" and "Through the

Panama"—both of which have received high praise and people write me about them all the time and no one has criticised me or suggested I wronged Malcolm's work in any way.[5]

What Mrs. Lowry does not add is that she has been doing no more than every reader is invited to do—indeed every reader inevitably must select in accordance with his own preoccupations, as the eye selects from the visual field.

The radical new form of his latest novel was determined by Lowry's attempt to face directly his own psychic turbulence, and the paranormal phenomena which threatened his sanity but were also quite near the source of extra-ordinary powers of recall and of association. Mrs. Lowry, not herself apparently a "psychic" or "sensitive" person, has testified to the reality of these phenomena. Lowry was sometimes driven to wonder if he were some kind of human freak—a throwback to a more primitive type of man.

The different versions of the novel that survived may be compared with the different versions of Lowry offered by his friends. I have received many versions of some events, proferred by different people, each convinced that he, and he alone, knew the authentic Lowry. I have been told that I. A. Richards meant about as much to Lowry as the Bishops—and I have also had Richards' version. (Aiken was the link.) In life, Lowry seems to have been a chameleon. The Protean qualities of his life became the Protean qualities of his writing. For example, in writing to his father, he naturally used the religious language of his youth, a language they had in common. This is not hypocrisy, it is simply linguistic adjustment.

The early versions of *October Ferry* began at the point of embarkation. The ferry between two islands, inner and outer worlds, is the scene of a dream sequence which in a cancelled chapter (No. 34, entitled "The Chapel Perilous" but differing from the chapter so marked in the published version) attains the climax of terror and dread. It is headed by a quotation from T. S. Eliot, *The Hollow Men*:

> Shape without form, shade without colour,
> Paralysed form, gesture without motion.

At the top of each manuscript page, Lowry has written "God help me", "God give me strength" or "St. Jude, please help"—St. Jude being the saint of desperate and dangerous causes.

He faces the recent traumatic experience, which occurred whilst he was in hospital in July 1949, in which he was convinced that for a short time he had physically "died" and been resuscitated. This experience is also behind the unpublished fragment "The Ordeal of Sigbjørn Wilderness".[6]

In a vision or dream, Ethan Llewlyn sees himself and his wife to be drowning in a raging sea. The ordeal ends when Ethan is seized by a strong hand. It is that of the dead friend—here called Charley, in the printed text Peter Cordwainer whose presence recalls the Cambridge suicide of Lowry's friend, Paul Leonard Charles Fitte, for which Lowry felt a reviving remorse. The suicide had been part of the early lost novel *In Ballast to the White Sea* (1936), which was to have been, like *October Ferry*, "The *Volcano* in reverse"; it is allusively present in the title of *Dark as the Grave*, with its echo of Cowley's ode on *his* lost Cambridge friend, but in the intervening decade it does not appear to enter the imaginative work, nor perhaps Lowry's consciousness.

Here, however, Charley[7] enters into a dream dialogue, bantering, free and affectionate, with his friend, telling him not to feel guilty because he, Charley, not wishing to take full responsibility for his own death, had quite knowingly goaded his friend into the taunts which spurred him on the final act. "Then I *am* your murderer" cries Ethan; but the ghost replies that if Ethan now commits suicide himself, keeping his word to "follow" his friend, he (Charley) will in turn be confined for ever by his own sense of guilt to the torments which he now endures.

Charley wants to leave with Ethan a thought which he transmits telepathically, not in words. It is that Ethan's unhappy childhood had been a punishment for sins committed in a past life, but as a man, having expiated his past, he will be permitted to re-enter the joys of childhood and to enjoy all previously withheld from him.

With the help of a ghost and of a kind giant with the face of Christ (?Kristbjorg, the name of the narrator of "In the Black Hills") Ethan and his wife are drawn from the engulfing waters. The final adjuration of the ghost as he disappears "And don't lose your sense of humour" serves as reminder, if the reader needs one, of Lowry's balance and sanity in the midst of his Satanic world. In the published version, the impulse to suicide on the ferry is brief, direct and speedily mastered. Whilst the apparition at the railroad crossing, as it appears in the published version, shows more of the "purely narrative and surface interest" that Albert Erskine asked for, the alternative version, with the weedy remnants of "The Ordeal of Sigbjørn Wilderness" still adhering to it, elucidates that ritual of childish play in "The Bravest Boat" which some have found sentimental (for *October Ferry* was originally designed for the collection of short stories, and Lowry observed that *October Ferry* and *Hear Us O Lord* together form "another kind of novel" [*Selected Letters*, p. 338]). He also wrote in "Work in Progress" that the author's own attitude is traditionally Catholic (not conformist):

> and in fact this attitude, if it succeeds eventually in being consciously expressed in its complexity is both more isolated and more "a voice crying in the wilderness" yet more universal than at first seems to be the case. . . . Even prophecies do not stand still, and any truth one might utter perhaps becomes untrue the moment it is voiced. . . .

The multiple versions of *October Ferry* and the complex levels of consciousness and dissociation for the protagonist represent another way to integration than the composite group of *Hear Us O Lord*. Alternative narrations, the "fishnet" form of construction, working through gaps, in each represents the necessary vehicle for "a battle between life and delirium in which life . . . is fighting to give that delirium a form"; and "Joyce has surely left some regions to explore, even to blaze the trail in those he didn't explore himself."[8]

The French translation, *En route vers l'île de Gabriola*, brings out the central theme very clearly, and, even in the act of stating the difficulties, quite explicitly:

> *Comment parler de ces impressions fugaces, reliées d'une manière vague mais certainement à une ordre mystérieux au delà de cette vie, concernant néanmoins cette vie, mais trop subtile pour s'articuler en clair? À les formuler en terms de rapport entre nous et le surnatur a l, rapporte qui peut, soit nous inciter à exécuter notre dessein, soit nous empêcher, nous risquons l'accusation de ridicule, sinon de quelque simplesse d'esprit. William James ne nous le cache point; un peu de plus, cette croyance conduit à l'obsession, à la demance, croyance qui, sans doute— cela aussi a été dit—suppose une méthode de pensée primitive que le civilisé a la réputation d'avoir largement éludée.*[9]

The English fumblings after something which perhaps only Indians know (one thinks of a collection of their utterances such as Teresa McLuhan's *Touch the Earth*) enable Ethan to reach consolation "when we most need help, which is almost the same as saying when we need assurance our lives are not valueless". This is translated ". . . *et cela spécialement lorsque nous avons besoin d'aide, de sorté que notre besoin de sécurité s'accroit avec la valeur conférée à nos vies*" (p. 349).

In *October Ferry* no words are final, the form cannot "freeze". An adumbration of Lowry's intentions, however clearly they may emerge from the notes and comments, does not ensure success; the blueprint cannot guarantee the finished product.

The anguish of *October Ferry* lies in the recognition that Paradise is no permanent place, that what is loved must be recognized to be transient. To surrender all this, in recognition that the eternal form lies elsewhere, asks a ritual of mourning; for the truest mirror of eternity reflects the outrage of time and change, whether in a loved home, in a landscape, in a marriage or in the final form of a work of art. Lowry renounces the idols not only of his life but also of his art.

The composite form of *Hear Us O Lord* is more traditional and safer. Joseph Conrad, whose influence on Lowry was profound, in his last collection of tales *Twixt Land and Sea* offered as he observed in a prefatory note, "the mingled subjects of civilization and wilderness, of land life and life on the sea" not as a preconceived plan. "It just happened by drawing from sources profounder than the logic of a deliberate theory suggested by acquired learning . . . or by lessons drawn from analysed practice." Eliot used the same method for his poetic sequences.

> It originated out of separate poems. . . . Then gradually I came to see it as a sequence. That's one way—doing things separately and then seeing the possibility of fitting them together, attuning them and making a whole of them. (Interview, *Paris Review*, spring–summer 1959, Number 21)

Hear Us O Lord is "attuned" by the underlying music of the fisherman's hymn which gives the title, and by the canon *Frère Jacques* which recurs throughout the book. *October Ferry* also has its hymn "Watchman, what of the night?" which Ethan sings jubilantly as the ship prepares to berth—"Hooray, the harbour's near / Lo the red light"; but which he also has seen pinned up in the ferry office.

In this work Lowry combined and superimposed many levels of his own lifestory. The burning of the Llewelyn's ancestral home conflates the burning of Lowry's waterside home in June 1944 (after which he fled not from, but to Niagara-on-the-Lake) and the concern he felt about agreeing to the sale of his old home Inglewood, to which, as one of his mother's heirs, he had given consent in 1951.[10]

Niagara-on-the-Lake, "the most beautiful town in Canada", becomes a setting for cosmic violence, from some poltergeist whose fires symbolize the war years, but intermingled with the natural thundery weather of a Lake Ontario summer. The whole region is reflected in a way at once fantastic and precise, with an accurate use of those few hundred square yards at the town centre, where the Prince of Wales Hotel (1864) faces the old court house (seat of the first Canadian parliament) and the Library, in which Ethen discovered horrendous psychic material. The clock tower, however, is not old, as in the novel, but a war memorial of this century; but the lake shore, the neighbouring town of Ixion (St. Catherine's) in a species of dream sequence reflect the two homes and what ejection from each has meant. This theme is peculiarly Canadian, and most powerfully effects the union of inner and outer worlds.

The idyllic final tale of *Hear Us O Lord* depicts the waterside home near Vancouver from which, in *October Ferry*, exile is decreed. The narrator is himself a musician. Not only does he use the wordless communication of a symphony, he also embarks on an opera—to be called "The Forest Path to the Spring". This story of a Wise Fool, rather like that Parzifal of whom Lowry's Cabbalist friend Charles Stansfeld-Jones wrote a study, is carefully planned in eight sections. The presiding poet is Wordsworth ("Love had he found in huts where poor men lie") and the style suggests something almost as conscious as Wordsworth's experiments in *Lyrical Ballads*.

When taunted by passing boatmen, the narrator is capable of the erudite rejoinder—in this case, "holophrastic"—but in general he uses what the Greeks termed the *"kai"* style, phrases linked by "and . . . and . . . and . . .". It is the style used by children but

151

also by the great jazzmen; the effect is to stress the musical element and to give a unified sweep analogous to that of Bob Dylan:

> How many roads must a man walk down
> Before you can call him a man?
> Yes 'n' how many seas must a white dove sail
> Before she can sleep in the sand? . . .,
>> The answer, my friend, is blowin' in the wind,
>> The answer is blowin' in the wind.

The wind that blew through the whole volume, the "Aeolian" sound expressed in a great variety of styles, culminates in this story; the magic journey of the Forest Path to the Spring is inexhaustible ("no wonder mystics have a hard task describing their illuminations") but "I dreamed that my being had been transformed into the inlet" (p. 269). "Though this part is an idyll it has to be remembered they were surrounded on all sides by the diabolic machinery of the volcano" wrote Lowry in "Work in Progress". In fact the calendar of events can be followed precisely in the tale, and in his life, from August 1940, when the Lowrys arrived in Dollarton, to the acquisition of their second home, where they moved on 1 May 1941 (as described in Section VI of the tale). This house was burnt down with many of Lowry's manuscripts in it on 6 June 1944 as described very briefly at the end of Section VII, but was later rebuilt.

During these years Lowry had actually been writing the final version, the great version, of his masterpiece, *Under the Volcano*; he virtually finished it, and took it to Niagara-on-the-Lake, where the last touches were put on Christmas Eve 1944. The tragic story of his great novel is thus polarized with this idyll; as in the novel itself are reflected obliquely the horrors of the Second World War, although only by anticipation, for *Under the Volcano* is set in the thirties. Whilst his brothers and his nephew were fighting, Lowry remained in Eridanus, his Western paradise, transforming the interior and the outer horrors. "The Forest Path to the Spring" was written five years later. Lowry points out in "Work in Progress" how the simplicity of the fishermen acts "both as a debunking factor and a sort of chorus"; he quotes Sam

> "The heagles, how they fly in great circles! Nature is one of the most beautiful things I ever saw in my life. Have you seen the heagle yesterday?"

adding "Sam is to be seen as a ridiculous but kindly version of the sailor in Millais' picture of the boyhood of Sir Walter Raleigh, pointing to the beyond, which is the theme of the tale."

This idyllic scene is viewed from afar in *October Ferry*, the Satanic vision, yet no longer as Satanic as *Under the Volcano*. As W. H. New has observed, the directional associations of Neoplatonism are adapted to a specific geography[11]—that of the Gulf of Georgia—across which, as Lowry would have rejoiced to know, a bathtub race takes place annually, much drinking preceding the rowing of these novel craft, and more following at the conclusion.

At the end we approach the island but do not land. The story is left open. A glance at the map will show that Dollarton, the home from which the Llewelyns set out, Nanaimo, the port where they take the ferry, and Gabriola, their new home, are aligned, the East for the gods, West for the demons, Gabriola between.

In these latest works, Lowry's new form may be summed up as a concern for the relations between man and his world, other than the relations of precisely focused characters, a structure largely dependant on gaps and radically simplified, yet working backwards and forwards through a dislocated time-sequence. The writer is moving about within his own past work, so that previous stories and characters assume for him the status of a "second world", which he changes, redistributing the emphasis. In all this, Lowry is the heir not only of Joyce but of the later Joseph Conrad, who returned in *Chance* and *Victory* to the world of his early stories, but transformed it with new ambiguities and depths.

Of this I have written briefly elsewhere;[12] much remains to be developed. In a review of works on Conrad, dissenting from this view (for he admits he sees Lowry's books "as documents of dipsomania, not works of art"), W. W. Robson asks "If 'good' has to be used with inverted commas round it, has not literary criticism disappeared?" (*Times Literary Supplement*, 27 May 1977).

Lowry wrote of *October Ferry*:

> You might have to go to Genet . . . to find anything more extreme. So they say . . . it creates a kind of power in itself that . . . takes your mind off the faults of the story itself, which incidentally are of every kind—in fact it possesses perhaps not

one single conventional virtue of the normal story . . . I have to accept the possibility that you will consider it a total failure . . .

(*Selected Letters*, pp. 339–40)

If Conrad was a post-Joycean writer writing in a pre-Joycean world, Lowry too was anticipating forms that were recognized only later. I began by suggesting that perhaps the normal processes of establishing a single text do not really apply. Yet Lowry ventured to suggest for his latest work an epigraph from *The Woodlanders* of Thomas Hardy:

> And yet their lonely courses formed no detached design at all, but were part of the great pattern in the great web of human doings then weaving in both hemispheres from the White Sea to Cape Horn.

NOTES

My transcriptions from the Lowry MSS were made in haste during a brief stay at the University of British Columbia in June 1975. They suffered severely in the course of a journey across the Rockies, and have not been checked. It seemed to me that the interest of the material justified the risks involved in quotation.

1 In 1971 Judith O. Combs compiled a list of Lowry's MSS at this library (Ref. Pub. No. 42); but since then, besides the items mentioned above, much more has accrued.

2 Quoted by John Fletcher, *Directions in Literature*, 1968, p. 105.

3 *Selected Letters*, p. 157; *Les Lettres Nouvelles*, special Lowry number, Juillet—Août 1960; *Selected Letters*, p. 258.

4 Letter of 6 January 1954. I am indebted for this reference, to the unpublished Cambridge dissertation of Brian O'Kill.

5 Quoted in Douglas Day, *Malcolm Lowry: A Biography*, 1973, p. 438 (footnote).

6 In this work, the protagonist is visited by two figures from his Cambridge past—James Travers, Charlotte Haldane; there is a letter addressed to his tutor, Tom Henn, because he was an Irishman, and understood the psychic levels of existence. Curiously, Dr. Henn himself later underwent the experience of being resuscitated after a short period when his heart stopped, and vividly described his recollections.

7 Charlotte Haldane in her novel *I Bring Not Peace* calls this figure Carling. Was Fitte known to his friends by his third name, Charles, rather than his first?

8 These extracts from "Work in Progress" were copied by me in 1975, as were the passages from *October Ferry*, at a time when these works had not been sorted out and catalogued. I was enabled to see them by

the kindness of the librarian. By now, no doubt, they have been indexed.

9   Tr. Clarisse Frencillon, *Les Lettres Nouvelles* (Paris, 1972), pp. 348–9.
10 "Noblesse Obliged"—unpublished—tells of the impoverished baronet Sir Thomas selling Greasby Hall—yet contriving by his courtly manner to carry off meeting his obligations at a Canadian village store with the very smallest cheque "on account". In another story a peer named The Earle of Thurstaston appears; both Greasby and Thurstaston are villages in Wirral, near Lowry's old home.
11 See his "Introduction to Commonwealth Fiction", *Among Worlds* (Erin, Ontario, 1975), p. 120.
12 In *Joseph Conrad; a Commemoration*, ed. Norman Sherry, 1976.

8

Strange Poems of God's Mercy: The Lowry Short Stories

by T. E. BAREHAM

Hear Us O Lord From Heaven Thy Dwelling Place[1] stands at a crossroads in Lowry's output. From this point, down one broad highway, stretches the main vista of his work—the achievement of *Under the Volcano*, the promise and near-fulfilment of the posthumous novels. But down other dark sideroads which diverge from here, we can be led a pretty dance through the quirkishness, the personal allusions and the occult world of Lowry at his most obscure and introspective. All his work is inter-connected. This makes the volume richly rewarding for the Lowry specialist, but may be daunting for the reader who comes to him for the first time through *Hear Us O Lord*. The object of this essay is to provide some preliminary guide-posts to the tracks which cross the terrain of the Lowry short stories.

Much of the material in the collection was planned towards the novel-cycle which was to be called "The Voyage That Never Ends". Lowry was a compulsive starter rather than a diligent finisher of his material; the additions to *Under the Volcano* even in galley-proof show how the literary journey never did seem to end. He worked through an allusive inter-connecting thought-stream technique, whose patterns may not be immediately obvious to "normal" everyday logic. One must consider also whether the very nature of the triumph in *Under the Volcano* may contribute to the fact that nothing else Lowry wrote seems finished in such a way that it can stand alone in its own right. He became haunted by the spectre of a novelist who could not repeat his one success and who, increasingly, lived in a private world of self-created barriers and inhibitions. If the Consul's claim of the world in

Under the Volcano that "this is Hell" is true, it is irresistible to continue the quotation on Lowry's behalf with "nor am I out of it". The problems are unusual enough to justify an expository account of the short stories, both for the light they shed on the mind of a man living in his self-created inferno, and for the solutions to the dilemma which they offer—solutions offered nowhere else in his work, except in the last chapters of *October Ferry to Gabriola*, with which the material in the short stories has much in common. In structure and in ideas the short stories have much to tell us about Lowry as man and as artist, and about Man as Artist in a larger and less personal sense.

The formal arrangement of the material in *Hear Us O Lord* seems to have been planned and finally decided by Lowry—a point worth making since it is not always true of his posthumous writings. The publisher's note to the Penguin edition (1969) explains:

> (he) . . . had conceived of . . . (*Hear Us O Lord*) . . . as a unit, and had arranged the tales and short novels of which it consists in a kind of curve, so that each story had a bearing upon those on either side of it.
>
> (p. 7)

Such an arrangement is in itself of interest, suggesting dynamic links between artistic units normally regarded as self-contained. It offered a method by which a writer, struggling for a synthesis of the disparate fragments he worked upon, could sustain a larger design.

It is commonplace that meanings and inter-dependences of the layers of work in *Under the Volcano* are only revealed with successive readings. So it is true that the bearing of each story upon the others in *Hear Us O Lord* becomes clearer and richer as one assimilates the grand design through continuing study. The stories *are* a connected curve, but the parabolic logic of the collection as an entity, as virtually a new art form, is only comprehensible in the context of the author's preoccupations in earlier phases of his writing. Most of the material in *Hear Us O Lord* stems from the period between finishing *Under the Volcano* and the final visit to Europe in 1954. The concern with the struggle for "success" is therefore obvious enough and forms a major link between all the stories. The book is also about isolation, for Lowry went into self-exile, both cultural and spiritual. He was fiercely proud of that strange integrity which he felt he was thus preserving. Most of the men in *Hear Us O Lord* explore this side of their own natures and steel themselves to test their indivduality against the world outside their chosen territory. The level at which Lowry's "curve" traces and develops this struggle may not be the deepest in the book, but it is an important one. Sigbjørn Wilderness in "Through the Panama" (pp. 26–98) is on his way to Europe, the great testing-ground for a New World author. In "Strange Comfort Afforded by the Profession" the same character is visiting Italy on a Guggenheim Fellowship and experiencing a sense of dislocation which has a far greater importance than mere home-sickness. The novelist hero of "Elephant and Colosseum", the schoolmaster Fairhaven in "Present Estate of Pompeii", and the jazz-symphonist narrator of "The Forest Path to the Spring" are equally alien to the environment in which they are initially situated, though there is a steady growth through the stories towards the moment of reconciliation at the end of "The Forest Path".

This is the most obvious example of linkage and development between the stories. One gradually becomes aware of numerous others. In the opening story, "The Bravest Boat", the tiny balsa-wood craft becomes a symbol of the unquenchable spirit of love; questing, enduring, sustaining. This seems a far cry from "Gin and Goldenrod", the penultimate story, yet the latter is also about endurance; and now repentance and regeneration are added as additional spiritual signs of growth, whilst in "Present Estate of Pompeii" the contrasts of eternity and transcience—though lightly touched upon—give the story a place in the overall picture of spiritual pilgrimage.

Lowry's world was haunted, bedevilled, illuminated by what he saw as strange coincidence, parellelisms, and omens. He lived in a fetishistic world where dates and places, brief snatches of overheard conversation, advertising slogans, and phrases from foreign languages, seemed to form repetitive patterns which he shaped into the vertebrae of his art. Wilderness's fear of sailing on the seventh day of the month was Lowry's own,[2] but it is melted back into the texture and implication of the voyage in "Through the Panama" with all its Conradian and Coleridgean features, and back out again through the nearly autobiographical aspects of Wilderness's confused but hyper-sensitive mind:

Significance of sailing on the 7th. The point is that my character
Martin, in the novel I'm furiously trying to get a first draft of
(knowing damned well I'd never do any work on this voyage,
which is to last precisely 7 weeks), had dreaded starting a
journey on the 7th of any month. To begin with we were not
going to leave for Europe until January. Then the message comes
that our sailing has been cancelled and we'll have to take advantage of the *Diderot's* sailing on the 6th if we want to go at all.
But she doesn't—she sails on the 7th. Martin Trumbaugh's
really fatal date is November 15. So as long as we don't leave
Los Angeles on Nov. 15 for the long haul, all will be well. Why
do I say that? The further point is that the novel is about a
character who becomes enmeshed in the plot of the novel he has
written, as I did in Mexico. . . .

(p. 27)

November is, of course, the month of the Feast of the Dead in
Mexico, the month in which all the action of *Under the Volcano*
occurs. Naturally—or very unnaturally—they *do* leave Los Angeles
on the fifteenth, having picked up another passenger: . . . "his
name? Charon. Naturally" (p. 31). There is a puckish humour
here. Lowry can take his weird preoccupation with coincidence quite
seriously, and yet laugh at it and himself. *Hear Us O Lord* contains much of his best humour; his verbal acrobatics, his eye for
whimsy, and his sheer love of laughter. This irreverent and sometimes flippant writing can be disconcerting, though only a misreading of *Under the Volcano* can fail to detect the same traits
there. The element of consternation is calculated.

The stories which comprise the respective movements of
Lowry's suite for prose orchestra in *Hear Us O Lord* are full of
interlinking elements which help to explain and justify his curve.
His locations seem widely disparate at first: a municipal park in
seaboard British Columbia, a boat going through the Panama
Canal, post-war Italy, then British Columbia again. The curve
is of course present in this scheme. Yet the metaphorical setting
is always the same in his work—Hell close to Eden, not far from
the sea or from some natural cataclysm, where man's civilized
vileness and his innate dignity are at war. He may cry "Hear Us
O Lord From Heaven Thy Dwelling Place", but the burden is of
man striving to be heard from his own dwelling place. For Lowry
the dwelling place was a spiritual quest. Displaced between
Canada, Mexico, and Europe, under threat of eviction from his

159

shack on the Burrard Inlet, in voluntary exile from the companionship of nearly all his literary contemporaries, his insistence upon the search for an identity and for a point of stasis is not surprising. It certainly gives the work in *Hear Us O Lord* an overall coherence within which the individual stories do form a parabola. The journey starts and ends in British Columbia, though all the tales are counterpointing tension against relaxation, Europe against America, the artist against the charlatan, past against present, and the tactile façade of sanity against the imaginary world of phantasy. For even in mid-twentieth century Canada the supernatural will rub shoulders with a Shell tanker! Roderick Fairhaven, enduring an unwanted guided tour of Pompeii (which he hates), lets his mind spiral backwards to his Canadian home:

> . . . it was this walk through the woods and back that he particularly remembered now: the stillness in the forest, the absolute peace, the stars sparkling and blazing through the trees (high on a cedar his flashlight gleamed on the four watching shining timorous curious eyes of two racoons), the stillness, the peace, but also the sense of hurt, the anxiety because of the renewed talk that evening of the possibility of the railroad's coming through, or that the forest would be slaughtered to make way for auto camps or a subsection, so that their troubles had seemed all at once, or once again, like those of country folk in a novel by George Eliot, or Finnish pioneers in the sixties (or, as Primrose Wilderness had remarked bitterly, Canadians or human beings of almost any period): and the sense too of something else topsy-turvily all the wrong way; Roderick stood quietly on his porch a moment, listening to the conversation of the tide coming in, bringing distantly, shadowily, more luminously, an oil tanker with it. To him, standing on his porch, holding his book and flashlight, it was as if Eridanus had suddenly become, like ancient Rome, a theater of prodigies, real and imaginary. As though the white whale hadn't been enough, the four o'clock news report from Vancouver heard over the Wilderness radio had related this in renewed reports from 'several accredited sources' of the famous 'flying saucers' of that period which had been witnessed that very afternoon from several different points travelling over Eridanus itself, and a sworn statement by the Chief of Police 'now released for the first time to the public, that he had, while fishing with his son beyond Eridanus Port the previous Sunday, seen, cavorting there, a sea serpent.' Good

God! This was all hilariously, horribly funny, and Roderick could laugh again thinking about it now. But the truth was he wasn't really amused: these things taken together with his other deeper anxieties, agitated him with that kind of dark conviction of the monstrous and threatening in everything sometimes begotten by a hangover. And unable to fit these matters comfortably into the filing cabinet of a civilised mind it was as if willy-nilly he'd begun to think with the archaic mind of his remote ancestors instead, and the result was alarming to a degree. . . .

(pp. 181–182)

This sense of swirling movement, with people and places overlapping, is present throughout the book. Sometimes Lowry asks more indulgence of his readers, or presupposes more interest in his personal shibboleths than is strictly fair or feasible. To understand fully any of his later writing one must first understand all his other writing, and this makes for a closed circle where no ready means of access is offered. No casual reader will be aware that the re-iterative engine song of the boats in *Hear Us O Lord* echoes back through most of his other books:

Frère Jacques!
Frère Jacques!
Dormez-vous?
Dormez-vous?
Sonnez les matines
Sonnez les matines
Ding dang dong,
Ding dang dong.

No Lowry character travels anywhere without hearing this refrain. It comes from the author's own merchant-seaman days and all the imaginative processes which originate in his undergraduate voyage to the Far East as an able seaman. One fictional reflection is straight back into "Elephant and Colosseum" where the hero makes a similar voyage to the China Sea, befriending a young elephant who becomes a symbol of redemption from the absurdities of artistic introspection when he re-meets her in Rome zoo twenty years later. The story is witty and finely realized. Yet it is only in its proper place, between "Strange Comfort" and "Present Estate" that its full significance will be recognised.

There is a fascinating mélange of fact, fancy, and wish fulfilment behind the surface of this and most of the short stories. "Elephant and Colosseum" is "made up", for its hero, Cosnahan, is a Manx-man, author of a supposed comic masterpiece. Yet the real interest is inwards, towards what we can learn about Lowry and about mankind at large, whilst so little does it matter *who* is telling the story in "Through the Panama" that we are presented with a situation where Sigbjørn Wilderness and Martin Trumbaugh (author and character) speak almost indistinguishably, and the voices of Lowry himself, of a guide book to the Panama, and of a parody of Coleridge's *Ancient Mariner*, interpose across the direction of the narrative flow. Lowry makes fresh and imaginative use of the device of marginal commentary which Coleridge had employed in his poem, in order to remind us that his hero is a Modern Mariner going his own strange and haunted voyage of discovery. Yet the casual reader, or a student coming to this book as his first Lowry, would have no means of knowing this, or of seeing the linkages between this story and so much else Lowry wrote. That "Frère Jacques" of the engines provides the link, as it alters in pitch, intensity, and implication. At one moment it becomes *Frère Jacques, frère Jacques, frère Jacques Laruelle"*. Laruelle is the Consul's friend/brother/alter ego/destroyer in *Under the Volcano*. This covert evocation of Lowry's masterpiece, which had cost him such herculean efforts, communicates a special atmosphere of tension to those who are able to pick up the reference. It must otherwise seem a very pointless piece of verbal foolery. At another moment the chant becomes . . .

> *Sonnez les matines*
> *Sans maison,*
> *Sans maison.*

and the fear of eviction, of a repetition of the fire that made the Lowrys homeless, and of all the associated traumas, rises through the other webs of plot to tug at the consciousness of the informed reader. *"Sonnez les matines"* becomes *"Sonnez lamentina"* as they pass down the coast of Mexico where the Consul had heard the bells of Oaxaca tolling *"Dolente, dolore"*.

The Manx fisherman's hymn from which *Hear Us O Lord* takes its title provides another linking motif. Lowry had a special affection for this hymn, and for its tune, "Peel Castle", "with its booming minor chords" (as he puts it in "The Forest Path to the Spring", p. 223):

. . . in which sounds all the savagery of the sea yet whose words of supplication make less an appeal to, than a poem of God's mercy.

That phrase itself is repeated later, when the narrator of "The Forest Path" speaks of his opera—here clearly an artistic equivalent of Lowry's novels:

> . . . I composed this opera, built, like our new house, on the charred foundations and fragments of the old work and our old life. The theme was suggested probably by my thoughts of cleansing the purgation and renewal and the symbols of the canister the ladder and so on, and certainly by the inlet itself, and the spring. It was partly in the whole-tone scale, like *Wozzeck*, partly jazz, partly folksongs or songs my wife sang, even old hymns, such as Hear Us O Lord From Heaven Thy Dwelling Place. I even used canons like Frère Jacques to express the ships' engines or the rhythms of eternity; Kristbjorg, Quaggan, my wife and myself, the other inhabitants of Eridanus, my jazz friends, were all characters, or exuberant instruments on the stage or in the pit. The fire was a dramatic incident and our own life, with its withdrawals and returns, and what I had learned of nature, and the tides and sunrises I tried to express. And I tried to write of human happiness in terms of enthusiasm and high seriousness usually reserved for catastrophe and tragedy.
>
> (p. 274)

There is a proud, articulate dignity about this claim which justifies the experiment in *Hear Us O Lord*, even where the attempt is not a total success. It *may* fail when the nature of linkages in ideas becomes too personal. One must also confess that there are moments when the volume fails because the quality of the writing is defective. The sentences run excitedly, but without control, several feet in front of the point Lowry's brain has got to, and his syntax can break down into a gauche, fifth-form-essay kind of enthusiasm; there is a descriptive passage on p. 261 of the Penguin text which is typical of this indiscipline. Two gargantuan sentences occupy thirty-two lines of prose during which time there are more than twenty repetitions of the conjunction "and". What happens is that as Lowry's form pushes at the boundaries of normal practice, so there is an inevitable accompanying strain upon the prose itself. He was seeking methods other than that of disjunctive thought-streaming to convey the processes and timbre

163

of interior monologue, and neither time, nor the pressure of his own emotional excitement, allowed for a cool reflective period of reassessment. So much of the work in the book is interior monologue rather than descriptive prose, that the wonder is rather at the small amount of error than otherwise.

These "strange poems" are, then, work in progress, they are *"études"* rather than sonatas, but they present a rich and stimulating challenge. I hope that this survey of links in the form of the book may explain the "strange" of my chosen title. Yet, however strange, they *are* poems. Appropriately, the first and the last of them, the shortest and the longest, are the most poetic— introit and vesper to the main curve of the work. "The Bravest Boat", with which the collection opens, sounds the theme of questing, of man's balance with nature, and of ghosts to be exorcised. Its tone is lyrical—almost too much so. Its themes are developed and expanded in each of the following stories, made more comic or heroic as the case may be. Yet the spirit of the balsa-wood boat with its sealed-in message of love and its indomitable but covert purpose suffuses the entire collection. It is a poem of mercy, assuredly, for the boat survives twenty years of storm-tossing before being rescued to unite Sigurd and Astrid. The scale and dimensions change in "Through the Panama", yet the same themes are discernible in that boat journey—a transmutation of Lowry's voyage to Europe. In "Strange Comfort" the wife-figure is absent, and hence the questing and yearning can be given a fresh aspect. The artistic and the personal desires and phobias blur and mix in this story, and in the end it is a sense of humour which allows Sigbjørn to recover his balance. Quizzical though it may be, and in itself tangential and fragmentary, this story assumes its proper meaning when seen as part of a pattern and a curve.

"Elephant and Colosseum" takes the love and alienation themes even further. The deracinated writer is now Kennish Drumgold Cosnahan, a Manxman livng in America, but visiting Italy to supervise the publication of a translation of his novel. This novel is supposed to recall his experiences as a sailor, when he nursed and grew to love a young elephant destined for Rome zoo. The encounter of man and beast is an epiphany for Cosnihan: his attempt to locate the translators of his precious book has been a farce, he has lost contact with his brothers, and just learned of the death of his mother. Yet all his tensions are released in the pure joy of the shared contact:

> But it was not from the knowledge that he would now work again
> —though he would—that his deepest satisfaction sprang, that
> was now making him feel as happy as—why, as happy as some
> old magician who had just recovered his powers and brought off
> a masterstroke!
>
> The words had almost slipped out of his mouth. And suddenly,
> at the realization of what he meant, a pure delight in all its
> renewed and ludicrous implications got the better of him, so that
> Cosnahan laughed aloud.
>
> Good God, he really *was* a magician. Or this was the real wild
> fount of his feeling, shared suddenly, human (at the same time
> more than just universally ancestral), though it seemed to be;
> this was the real antique and secret source of his present pride,
> of his future salvation; this that would have caused his book to
> be translated, and by that, more than that, himself to be trans-
> lated—his mother's son at last—into a conscious member of the
> human race.   (p. 174)

"Present Estate of Pompeii" pursues the theme of opposition between Old and New World values, with all its accreted "meanings".[3] It certainly offers an investigation of the motif of love from a new angle, since the guide, appropriately named Signor Salacci, seems to have a mono-maniacal preoccupation with the sex life of the ancient and ruined city. The symbolic potential looms large, but Lowry's touch is light and deft. The story leads, with no need of a physical return journey, back to British Columbia. "Gin and Goldenrod" extends some of the ideas implicit in "Present Estate of Pompeii", but it is rich enough to add many more. In "Gin and Goldenrod" one of the best written and best directed stories in the collection, the narrative line emerges tangentially. This technique of making narrative exposition subsidiary to, but a part of, character description, is one of Lowry's contributions to the art of fiction. Sigbjørn Wilderness has been on a "bender" at a sordid little villa where the owner has been selling bootleg liquor to Sunday drinkers. Sigbjørn is now obliged to make a penitential return journey to pay the debts incurred during his binge. The day is hot, the road dusty, and the countryside ravaged by building developments which are encroaching onto the natural forestland of the Wilderness's home—their surname, of course, is no accident. This desolation of abomination is, on one level, the New World counterpart of Pompeii, the inversion being perfect, yet the analogy exact. The story is again about spiritual atrophy, about lack of love and confidence. Primrose Wilderness, half reproving, half supporting, accompanies her husband. Though the bond of sympathy has been strained by his behaviour, her love and purpose are able to transcend the horror of the moment. Even amidst the debris of the new building lots she seeks tokens of nature to refresh, revitalize, and encourage the disconsolate man by her side. The gin and the goldenrod of the story's title are to be seen as symbols of the opposing ways of life open to Sigbjørn. The entire book is about this opposition, and about the power of love (if one can find and hold it) to effect a balance between them. "Turn this into triumph: the furies into mercies . . ." notes Wilderness to himself with regard to his projected novel ("Through the Panama", p. 27). This suggests the creative artist as magician, and recalls Cosnahan's moment of truth,[4] and the bravest boat which, mysteriously, through its message of love, survived the furious seas and united Sigurd and Astrid.

In "The Forest Path to the Spring" the transmutation of furies into mercies takes final and definitive shape. Although its narrator is a musician who has lost his *magnum opus* (a symphony) in a fire and has now turned to opera instead, he is clearly akin to Lowry himself, who after the loss of *In Ballast to the White Sea* in the conflagration which destroyed his first hut at Dollarton, turned to rather different prose kinds—as in "The Forest Path" itself. Through the semi-autobiography are woven all the preoccupations which inform Lowry's work: the relationship of man to nature, to other men, to himself; the value and durability of art; the causes and effects and the mysterious ways of God's mercy to his creatures. And it is an affirmation of the joy of living. Readers who know only *Under the Volcano* often misjudge Lowry. Despite his desperate moods of depression and his moments of panic and despair, he was not an habitually gloomy man. "The Forest Path" shows how he was able to subsume the ordinary and the visionary moments of his life into a pattern—to be a larger and more creative being, for instance, than is Geoffrey Firmin in *Under the Volcano*. Firmin's is the courage of despair, and this was not Lowry's mood for much of the time in those Canadian years, despite the hardships of life in the wild. The last words of the final story in the collection are, "Laughing we stooped down to the stream and drank" (p. 287). Nothing could be more fulfilled than this, both in the physical context, and through all the meanings which "spring" in both its senses takes on in the story. Here man and nature have found a perfect equipoise. The act of living has become an act of faith, and this is enough in itself.

The curve is complete. As the book began with two lovers brought together by the magical sea changes of "The Bravest Boat", so it ends where spring and sea meet, and where two lovers have worked out their own salvation, where the magic comes from within. It began in a park where the lynx "in which seemed to be embodied in animal form all the pure ferocity of nature" (p. 20) is caged, prowling and pacing endlessly. It ends with the author facing a mountain lion in the lovely wilderness which surrounds his home. The animal is real enough, yet it is also a representation of the untamed, self-destructive side of his own nature, as he goes his peaceable path to the spring for water. Moments of a Wordsworthian despair have crippled him, even here in the forest, and the lion appears at the worst of these crises. So again man is faced by pure untamed nature, at once brutal and beautiful. It is his own courage, his instinctive grasp upon life, which now effects a purgation beyond reason or conscious will:

> So I stood traditionally and absolutely still. Then we simply waited, both of us, to see what the other would do, gazing straight into each other's eyes at short range; in fact it was only his gleaming topaz eyes and the tip of his tail twitching almost imperceptibly that showed me he was alive at all.
>
> Finally I heard myself saying something like this to the mountain lion, something extraordinary and absurd, commanding yet calm . . . 'Brother, it's true. I like you in a way, but just the same, between you and me, get going!' Something like that. The lion, crouched on a branch really too small for him, caught off guard or off balance, and having perhaps already missed his spring, jumped down clumsily, and then, overwhelmed, catlike, with the indignity of this ungraceful landing, and sobered and humiliated by my calm voice—as I liked to think afterwards— slunk away guiltily into the bushes . . . (p. 265)

There is a metaphysical link between the beasts of first and last stories, which follows the curve of the intervening narratives, and to which the albatross of "Through the Panama" and the elephant of "Elephant and Colosseum" are united. This and other cyclic patterns, the alienation motif, the theme of redemption, the power of humour to restore the balance of life, and the value of love, makes *Hear Us O Lord* a remarkable and moving book, whilst the smaller arabesques within each story ensure that the themes do not become merely repetitive. "Strange" they may be, but assuredly they are "poems" and, triumphantly, poems of God's mercy.

NOTES

1 All references to the text of *Hear Us O Lord From Heaven Thy Dwelling Place* are to the edition by Penguin Books, 1969. Within the essay this title is shortened to *Hear Us O Lord*.

2 In "The Bravest Boat" Sigurd and Astrid have been married seven years and Astrid found Sigurd's message when she was seven. In both *Dark as the Grave wherein my Friend is Laid* and *October Ferry to Gabriola* this same hyper-sensitivity to numerical coincidence can be seen.

3 This story also seems to introduce the drink problem, which is common to Lowry and to most of his heroes. I feel the motif is perhaps not strongly enough brought to the fore in "Present Estate". It provides the obvious link forward to "Gin and Goldenrod" of course.

4 Cosnahan's mother had powers which earned her the reputation of being a witch. The magician figure is also present in *October Ferry* and, more obscurely, in Juan Fernando Martinez, the "friend" of *Dark as the Grave wherein my Friend is Laid*. Since Fernando, was created out of the same character as Dr. Vigil in *Under the Volcano*, the "occult" links between books can again be seen spreading outwards here.

Notes on Contributors

T. BAREHAM is a graduate of Lincoln College, Oxford, and is a senior lecturer in English at the New University of Ulster. He has published on a wide range of subjects; Shakespeare, Dekker, Garth, Blackmore, and Malcolm Lowry. He is the author of *George Crabbe* (1977) and is co-author, with Simon Gattrell, of a bibliography of Crabbe (1977).

M. C. BRADBROOK was Mistress of Girton College, Cambridge, until her retirement in 1976. She is the author of many books on Elizabethan drama and poetry, and has published books on Marvell, Conrad, Ibson, Eliot, as well as a study of *Malcolm Lowry* (1974). Her recent work includes a book on Shakespeare, to be published by Weidenfield and Nicolson in September 1978; an essay on Marvell in a book of commemorative essays to be published in the U.S. by Archon Press; a lecture on Marvell, given at the Hull University tercentenary celebration, to appear in a collection of the lectures given on that occasion, edited by R. L. Brett (O.U.P., 1978), and an introduction to the new Everyman edition of Virginia Woolf's *To The Lighthouse*.

RICHARD HAUER COSTA wrote the first full study of Lowry in 1972. He earlier published a study of H. G. Wells (Twayne, 1967) and has completed a memoir of Edmund Wilson. He teaches fiction at Texas A & M University, and edits *Quartet*.

PERLE EPSTEIN received her degree in Comparative Literature from Columbia University. She is the author of *The Private Labyrinth of Malcolm Lowry* (197–) and has written several other books on mysticism and related topics. Her most recent book, *KABBALAH: The Way of the Jewish Mystic* has just been released by Doubleday. She is currently at work on a book about her own experiences in the world of the mystics.

169

SHERRILL GRACE is Assistant Professor of English at the University of British Columbia and has published articles on Lowry and on Canadian literature. Professor Grace currently holds a Canada Council Research Grant to continue the study of Expressionism in North American literature. She has recently completed a study of Lowry, *The Voyage That Never Ends*.

BRIAN O'KILL is formerly a scholar of Trinity College, Cambridge, and wrote his doctoral dissertation at Cambridge on Lowry's use of language. He is now Senior Research Editor of the revision of Halkett & Laing, *A dictionary of anonymous and pseudonymous publications in the English language*, the first volume of which will be published in 1978.

STEPHEN TIFFT is a graduate of the University of East Anglia, and teaches at Cornell University.

GEORGE WOODCOCK edited *Canadian Literature* from its foundation in 1959 until 1977. He has edited *Malcolm Lowry: The Man and His Work*, and published *The Crystal Spirit: A Study of George Orwell, Anarchism*, and *Herbert Read: The Stream and the Source*. His most recent publication is *Peoples of the Coast*.

Index

Achad, Frater, 131
Aiken, Conrad, 21, 35, 38, 40, 87–9, 97n., 147
Alain-Fournier, Henri, 81
Allen, Walter, 40
Atwood, Margaret, 146

Balázs, Béla, 94
Bang, Hermann, 95
Barlach, Ernst, 94, 99
Barzun, Jacques, 35
Bergson, Henri, 79, 97n.
Besant, Annie, 83
Birney, Earle, 39, 43, 144
Blackmur, R. P., 30
Blake, William, 140
Blamires, Harry, 43
Boden, Capt. Lyon and Mrs., 19
Bradbrook, M. C., 11, 16, 40
Brooke-Rose, Christine, 38
Brown, Leonard, 30
Bunyan, John, 53–4
Burgess, Anthony, 40
Burnet, Thomas, 54

Cabinet of Dr. Caligari, The, 96, 102, 104–5, 106, 107, 108
Calder-Marshall, Arthur, 85
Camus, Albert, 141
Cape, Jonathan, 34, 90, 119, 145
Cary, Joyce, 31
Celine, Louis-Ferdinand, 33
Chandler, Raymond, 33
Chaucer, Geoffrey, 27

Coleridge, S. T., 158, 162
Combs, Judith O., 144n.
Connolly, Cyril, 85
Conrad, Joseph, 150, 153–54, 158
Cowley, Abraham, 148
Cowley, Malcolm, 79
Crane, Hart, 39

Dante, 37, 55, 59, 112, 113, 118, 120, 122–23, 130, 131
Day, Douglas, 34, 40, 41–2, 47–8, 125, 146
Descartes, 138
Dos Passos, John, 35
Dostoevsky, Fyodor, 29, 94–5
Dunne, J. W., 79
Durrell, Lawrence, 41
Dylan, Bob, 152

Edmonds, Dale, 32, 41
Edschmid, Kasimir, 96–7
Eisner, Lotte, 103
Eliot, T. S., 147, 150
Epstein, Perle, 56
Erskine, Albert, 75, 144, 146, 149
Everson, William, 102
Expressionist Cinema, 93–111, 118
Expressionist Movement, 94–7

Fallada, Hans, 100
Faulkner, William, 79–81, 86–8
Fitte, Paul Leonard Charles, 148
Fitzgerald, F. Scott, 39, 104n.
Flecker, James Elroy, 116

171

Flint, R. W., 36
Fort, Charles, 83
Fowles, John, 146
Françillon, Clarisse, 113, 149n.
Frye, Northop, 48, 59
Furness, R. S., 101

Gass, William, 41
Gibbs, Philip, 35
Goethe, 57–9, 64, 100
Gogol, Nikolai, 80–1
Grace, Sherrill E., 97n., 99n., 144
Greene, Graham, 33
Greig, Nordahl, 21, 85
Gustafson, Ralph, 126

Haig-Brown, Roderick, 113–14
Haldane, Charlotte, 148n.
Hammett, Dashiel, 33
Hands of Orlac, The, 102, 105, 106
Hardy, Thomas, 154
Heilman, Robert B., 36–8, 42
Helmetag, Charles, 94n.
Hemingway, Ernest, 32, 39, 85
Hudson, W. H., 113–14

Isherwood, Christopher, 85

Jackson, Charles, 33–4
James, Henry, 80n., 90
James, William, 56
Johnson, Elizabeth, 72n.
Josipovici, Gabriel, 82–3
Joyce, James, 30, 35, 36, 40, 43, 144, 149, 153
Jung, Carl Gustav, 95, 118–19

Kafka, Franz, 94, 99
Kaiser, Georg, 95, 99, 102
Keyserling, Herman, 83
Kilgallin, Tony, 54n.
Knickerbocker, Conrad, 40
Kokoschka, 94, 102

Lawrence, D. H., 85n.
Leavis, F. R., 85n.
Leys Fortnightly, 17
Lipski, Jan Joseph, 98

Locke, John, 138
London, Jack, 110n.
Lost Weekend, The, 33–4
Lowry, Arthur O., 11, 18, 19, 21, 22, 23–4, 26
Lowry, Evelyn, 22
Lowry, Malcolm (works discussed):
    "The Bravest Boat", 149, 158, 164, 167; Dark as the Grave Wherein My Friend Is Laid, 83, 93, 117, 124, 126, 127, 146, 148, 158n.; "Elephant and Colisseum", 158, 161–62, 164–65, 168; "Enter One in Sumptuous Armour", 24; "The Forest Path to the Spring", 29, 85, 112, 113–14, 115, 124, 125, 128, 130–43, 146, 151–52, 158, 162–63, 166–68; "Ghostkeeper", 69n.; "Gin and Goldenrod", 158, 165–66; Hear Us O Lord From Heaven Thy Dwelling Place, 39, 109, 125, 145, 149, 150–51, 156–68; "Hotel Room in Chartres", 30n.; In Ballast to the White Sea, 59n., 124, 148, 166; "In the Black Hills", 145, 148; "I've Said Goodbye to Shanghai", 18; "June the 30th, 1934", 100–1; "Lament", 123; "La Mordida", 117, 124; "The Light that Failed Not", 80; Lunar Caustic, 59n., 84, 102, 104–5, 146; "Marching Down the High Road to China", 18; "Noblesse Obliged", 151n.; October Ferry to Gabriola, 97n., 103, 107, 108–9, 124, 126–27, 144–55, 157, 158n., 166n.; "On Board the West Hardaway", 30n.; The Ordeal of Sigbjørn Wilderness, 148–49; "The Present Estate of Pompeii", 158, 160–61, 165; "Strange Comfort Afforded by the Profession", 158, 161, 164; "Tender is the Night" (filmscript), 104n.; "Through the Panama", 38, 39, 147, 158–59, 162, 164, 166, 168; Ultramarine, 19, 27, 30, 33, 100, 102, 104n., 115–16, 121; Under the Volcano,

11, 18, 29–92, 93, 94, 97–109
passim, 130, 144–45, 148, 152–53,
156–57, 159, 162, 166; *The Voyage
that Never Ends*, 97, 109, 114,
156; "Work in Progress", 144,
145, 149, 152–53
Lowry, Margerie Bonner, 39, 126,
144, 146–47
Lowry, Russell (co-author of "I've
Said Goodbye to Shanghai" and
"Marching Down the High Road
to China"), 9–28 *passim*
Lowry, Stuart, 16, 17, 23–4
Lowry, Wilfrid, 10, 13–14, 15, 17

Maeterlinck, Maurice, 95
Marlowe, Christopher (*Dr. Faustus*),
37, 55, 57–8
McLuhan, Teresa, 150
Markson, David, 39, 42–3, 144
Melville, Herman, 32, 93
Milton, John, 112, 118, 128
Mitchell, Breon, 95n.
Munch, Edvard, 94–5, 101, 102

Nadeau, Maurice, 144
New, W. H., 43, 153

O'Kill, Brian, 146n.
O'Neill, Eugene, 95, 98, 99
Ortega y Gasset, J., 67–8, 145
Orwell, George, 85
Ouspensky, P. D., 83

Plomer, William, 34, 35
Poe, Edgar Allan, 95
Prairie Schooner (Lowry issue), 40
Proust, Marcel, 34–5, 114–15
Pyrrhus, 16, 18, 19

Read, Herbert, 96
Reed, Talbot Baines, 16
Remarque, Erich Maria, 33
Richards, I. A., 147
Rimbaud, Arthur, 56–7, 94, 95
Robbe-Grillet, Alain, 144
Robson, W. W., 153
Ruskin, John, 114, 128

Schopenhauer, Artur, 72
Schorer, Mark, 35
Shakespeare, 37, 60–6 *passim*
Sokel, Walter, 102
Spender, Stephen, 32, 34, 64n.
Spengler, Oswald, 95
Stansfeld-Jones, Charles, 83, 151
Stern, James, 113, 145
Sterne, Lawrence, 35
Strindberg, August, 94, 102
Swedenborg, Emanuel, 130

Thomas, Hilda, 113
Thoreau, Henry, 29, 113–14
Toynbee, Philip, 39–40

Ullman, Stephen, 81n.

Wain, John, 40
Weisstein, Ulrich, 96, 98
Whitman, Walt, 85n., 90
Wilde, Oscar, 95, 98
Willett, John, 94
Wilson, Edmund, 39
Wodehouse, P. G., 80
Wolfe, Thomas, 36, 39
Woodburn, John, 30–1, 35
Woodcock, George, 39, 72n., 93, 113
Wordsworth, William, 151, 167
Worringer, Wilhelm, 95